UNREDEEMED RHETORIC

UNREDEEMED RHETORIC

Thomas Nashe
and the Scandal of Authorship

Jonathan V. Crewe

The Johns Hopkins University Press
Baltimore and London

The Johns Hopkins University Press, Baltimore, Maryland 21218
The Johns Hopkins Press Ltd., London

Library of Congress Cataloging in Publication Data

Crewe, Jonathan V.
Unredeemed rhetoric.

Includes bibliographical references and index.
1. Nash, Thomas, 1567–1601–Criticism and interpretation.
2. Rhetoric–1500–1800.
I. Title.
PR2326.N3Z6   828'.309   82-6554
ISBN 0-8018-2848-1   AACR2

PR
2326
N3
.Z6

CONTENTS

PREFACE

In speaking of *rhetoric*, I have adopted a term that has, in one way or another, dominated modern discussions of Renaissance literature. The phenomenon, as well as the term, clearly preoccupied Renaissance authors, for reasons that have often been given. (They include the "rediscovery" on a large scale of classical rhetoric, the promotion of rhetoric as opposed to dialectic within the educational structure, the high valuation placed upon decorum in courtly settings, the moral force attributed to artful persuasion, and many others.) In the literature of the Renaissance, rhetoric is figured, benignly or otherwise, as protean, and its transformations fascinate virtually every major English author from Wyatt to Milton. Rhetoric is also "given" as a repertoire of effects to be exploited, a set of exercises to be performed, and a body of theory to be applied; perhaps even as a state of heightened consciousness in relation to language. It cannot be by-passed except—with dubious results—by the most extreme millenarians acting under the direct prompting of the spirit. The acceptance of rhetoric, whether as a form of good or as a necessary evil, virtually constitutes what we call Renaissance literature.

For my discussion I have, therefore, chosen an established critical theme as well as a conscious preoccupation of writers within the period I will consider. What remains to be shown is why another book on rhetoric is necessary. On that score my arguments must speak for themselves; yet I should like to narrow in advance the scope of my concern. I am not undertaking to define rhetoric, the protean nature of which makes it difficult to pin down; nor shall I attempt to write a chapter in the history of rhetoric, to add to the common understanding of rhetorical theory or technique, or to engage in rhetorical analysis. I am concerned with a perhaps ill-defined but enduring principle of rhetoric, a principle that embodies contradictions but that comes into being in the same moment a principle of strict logic asserts itself. It is this "philosophical" principle of rhetoric that I shall take, if not quite for granted, then at least as the inalienable basis of my discussion.

I shall also assume that in principle and in practice rhetoric is the irreducible foundation of style, of performance, and of literature in the Renaissance. It constitutes an origin that each of these may seek to transcend, yet it will in reality continue to determine all of them. Although "rhetoric" may appear in sublimated guises or with superstructural elaborations, it will never cease to be the fundamental principle of the various art forms I discuss. Nor will moments of tactical opposition between "style" and "rhetoric," for example, or between "poetry" and "rhetoric," alter the underlying continuity of rhetoric. There will, in other words, be no saving difference between "rhetoric" and its superimposed art forms. The validity of these assumptions remains to be justified by my discussion.

The question "Why another book about rhetoric?" may be easier to answer than the question "Why Nashe at all?" It will soon be evident that I am "using" Nashe, as he has been used in other contexts, to make a point. His work enables me to explore not what rhetoric essentially "is," but what the presence and availability of rhetoric entails for a Renaissance author. If Nashe really lends himself to such an exploration, it is partly because the highly "rhetorical" nature of his writing has always been recognized, but partly because he emerges as a significant if not always explicit commentator on the predicament of the "rhetorical" author. Instead of apologizing for using Nashe in this way, I will suggest that this is a way in which he has insufficiently been used.

I am not primarily concerned, then, with giving a full or circumstantial account of Nashe's career, nor are such accounts lacking. Nashe's work has been heroically edited and annotated, it has been adequately criticized, and its entertaining qualities have fully been appreciated. No injustice remains to be rectified, nor is it necessary to write about Nashe simply because he is there. It is of course possible that in reading Nashe I have misrepresented him, but in the case of so uncanonical an author the offense may be considered pardonable.

I am, however, concerned about the possible accusation that I have treated the chronology of Nashe's writings cavalierly, thus misrepresenting the shape of his career. To this I can only reply that the chronology of composition (as opposed to publication) cannot fully be determined. Moreover, Nashe's claim to have written a great deal suggests that some of his work may not have survived. The nature and extent of his collaborations is also not clear. I will therefore suggest that any strictly evolutionary (or other) shape imposed on Nashe's career is likely to be factitious. Although I have tried to respect the facts insofar as they are known, I have also claimed a certain freedom to dispose Nashe's highly opportunistic works according to the logic of my own argument. Any resulting errors may be rectified by a reader who will consult R. G. McKerrow's still-impressive edition of Nashe's works.

ACKNOWLEDGMENTS

It is a pleasure for me to record the debt I owe to many friends and former teachers, both at Berkeley and elsewhere. I recall with special thankfulness the stimulation, challenge, and academic cameraderie of Mark Seltzer, Joseph and Paula Carroll, John Coetzee, David Miller, and Joel Fineman. Most of those named worked their way through my tangled manuscript, gently insisting on clarification. Their own work supplied me with examples that I was more fully capable of admiring than of emulating. I also recall with special gratitude the example and support of Stephen Greenblatt, whose living engagement with Renaissance literature sets his work apart from so much that is only routine. I am not alone in having benefited from his unflagging enthusiasm and intellectual vitality. Paul Alpers made no secret of his distaste for Nashe, but generously overcame his misgivings in offering me his encouragement and advice. Randolph Starn gave me the benefit of his expertise as a Renaissance historian; he also subjected my work to his own friendly skepticism. It goes without saying that none of those named is responsible for the failings of this book. My greatest debt is owed to members of my family, whose endurance proved equal to the severe demands placed on it.

UNREDEEMED RHETORIC

CHAPTER 1

NASHE AND "RHETORIC"

Paradoxically, though Nashe's pamphlets are commercial literature, they come very close to being, in another sense, "pure" literature: literature which is, as nearly as possible, without a subject. In a certain sense of the word "say," if asked what Nashe "says," we should have to reply Nothing.—C. S. Lewis

It is fair, if simplistic, to say that the principal question usually asked of *The Unfortunate Traveller* is "What is it about?" Inquiries into its form, its structure, the nature and direction of its topical allusion, all return to uncertainty about its final concern. An inexplicable themelessness has been the real problem in almost all Nashe's writing.—R. A. Lanham

In this book, I shall take as given the "Nashe problem" defined in the two quotations that appear above.[1] Undoubtedly, questions are already begged—and historical explanations by-passed[2]—in taking as given Nashe's mysterious "themelessness." What interests me, however, is the plain fact that Nashe has recurrently presented himself in this baffling way to readers. Of course, it is not clear at once whether the problem is created by Nashe, by the act of reading as such, or by a particular way of reading. I would suggest that all three possibilities are involved, but I will not explore any one of them exclusively. What I shall suggest instead is that the problem arises because "theme" or "content" (saying something) are taken to be primary, while "writing" is taken to be secondary. Nashe appears inexplicably to reverse priorities, granting a constitutive autonomy to what can logically be only secondary or derivative. Theme, content, or meaning must come first; only after one of these is present can writing begin.

1

The presence of this assumption in my two opening quotations may make them sound old-fashioned. To that extent, a particular way of reading may be the "real problem." Under present critical assumptions, literariness virtually begins where "saying something" or being "about" something end. The "theme," while not wholly dismissed as an irrelevance, tends no longer to be assigned a constitutive status within the work, and the critic's task is not at an end when he has dissected out the theme. It has become possible, in fact, to regard the theme as a rhetorical device, or as the merely conventional pretext (the "red herring") that Nashe ultimately and self-consciously makes it. The theme, in other words, is not essentially at stake in the work; it is not the rational soul inhabiting the mere body of words, nor is it the center upon which the verbal structure rests secure. On the contrary, the *literary* work is always in excess of its specifiable theme, not economically proportioned to it. This excess at once lends itself to aesthetic appreciation and banalizes the theme.

Given all this, Nashe may be a less anomalous figure than he once appeared to be; he may even become a case in point, illustrating the nature of literariness. I shall, however, pursue the question of Nashe's themelessness a little further, partly because that perceived condition gives rise not only to appreciation or bafflement but to marked anxiety in the minds of certain readers. Furthermore, what Nashe represents in an extreme form characterizes to a lesser degree the work of his contemporaries. To consider the problem of reading Nashe is in some degree to consider that of reading the literature of his period, which of course includes the work of Shakespeare. (To what extent is the work of Shakespeare critically accountable in terms of its responsible "themes?" If Shakespeare is not fully accountable in such terms, what is the nature of the unreduced excess in his work?)

I shall also pursue the question of Nashe's alleged themelessness because, in the last resort, *themelessness* is a convenient term under which to approach an author who foregrounds performance as the irreducible and nonnegotiable characteristic of his own work, who accordingly cries out for appreciation, but who is nevertheless sufficiently conscious to attempt a continuous reckoning with the nature of his own performance, his own rhetorical predicament, and his own roles.[3] It is with this reckoning that I shall finally be concerned, but my immediate task is to take account of some reactions to Nashe.

What, then, is so peculiar about Nashe in the eyes of readers? It is not the limited partisanship Nashe inspires so much as the large uneasiness he provokes that first alerts us to the presence of a genuine issue in his work. To be more precise, critics who are drawn, sometimes obsessively, to Nashe may feel obliged to exonerate themselves from any blame, and to repudiate quite violently the tendencies he displays. Such critics may even oscillate between denying Nashe any power at all and asserting his power to corrupt.

That Nashe's elder contemporary Gabriel Harvey was the first and remains the best-known of his victims—his exemplary victim, even—may seem to prove little, since Harvey was directly provoked.[4] Yet it is worth pausing over Harvey's statement of his case:

> Alas, he is pitifully bestead, that in an Age of Pollicy, and in a world of Industry (wherein the greatest matters of Gouernement, and Valour, seeme small to aspiring capacities) is constrained to make woeful Greene, and beggarly Pierce Pennylesse, (as it were a Grashopper, and a Cricket, two pretty musitians, but silly creatures) the argumente of his stile.[5]

What is baffling—even, in other passages, to Harvey—is the fact of constraint. So too is Nashe's expropriation of the justifying "argument" to which Harvey's "stile" is, as he thinks, naturally entitled. The quarrel with Nashe not only made a fool of Harvey, but increasingly obsessed him, and culminated in the prohibition of both authors' works. Driven at one point to despair, Harvey abandons his condescension and reveals the underlying panic:

> Sweet Gentlemen, imagine it to be a speech, addressed vnto your selues. *Peraduenture the viper did neuer bite any of you; and the Gods forbid, it should euer bite you; but when you espie any such pernicious creature you presently dispatch it.* [2:37]

While none of Harvey's successors has ever matched him for anguished intensity, the paradox of the cricket and the serpent has implicitly recurred in subsequent criticism.

It is present in R. G. McKerrow's commentary, and far from diminishing the grandeur of his edition of Nashe, may be partly responsible for that grandeur.[6] Although there is no reason to dispute McKerrow's scholarly justifications for that edition, the editorial technique and apparatus come to provide an unassailable argument for trifling with the cricket,[7] and a certain judicial severity enters into McKerrow's dealings with the author.[8] McKerrow also rehabilitates the serious, "progressive" Gabriel Harvey, whom he compares favorably with his discreditable antagonist. Richard Lanham, convinced of Nashe's artistic failure, is still sufficiently alarmed by the reappearance of Nashe's alleged verbal excesses in certain (unnamed) writers of the twentieth century to issue a general alert.[9] Without ever ceasing to be regarded as a marginal or minor figure (the cricket), Nashe paradoxically remains a source of disproportionate, if intermittent, disturbance (the serpent).

It is not Nashe's status that is in question here so much as is a powerless frivolity at once presupposed and energetically reaffirmed, a frivolity that threatens continuously and paradoxically to "take over" and install itself in the ideal center:

> I would be loth to see the garden of Alcinous made the garden of Greene, or Motley. [2:38]

The cricket, the serpent, and now the motley fool; what is it that Harvey believes himself to be dealing with? Is it a form of evil the very troublesomeness of which lies in its instability? That cannot consistently be taken seriously or lightly, but that transforms itself in such a way as to baffle every attempt to stage a decisive confrontation? It is a peculiar but suggestive metamorphosis that transforms a cricket into a serpent, and it is equally peculiar that a figure of motley should have the power to take possession of the Garden of Alcinous, sacred to the recreation of heroes. From what does the power of motley derive?

If the characteristics we have so far encountered in Nashe criticism—including bafflement and contradiction—derive from a single cause with which the author is identified, that is the cause of "pure" rhetoric conceived from what we have learned to call a logocentric point of view. *Themelessness, verbal excess, nullity, marginality, scandalousness, and sinister encroachment* (to name only those for the present) are all terms invoked in the traditional moralistic critique of rhetoric, and it would be no surprise to find that pure rhetoric had been "always the real problem" in any discussion of Nashe. Even if it is not a "problem" to all, it is so viewed by Richard Lanham, whose history, like that of many critics within the field, is one of progressive entanglement in the "problem" of rhetoric.

Compulsively drawn to the problem, Lanham attempts a short cut. In *The Motives of Eloquence*,[10] he promotes "rhetoric" to the level of a countervailing principle, eternally opposed, in *concordia discors*, to "seriousness." Although the opposition of rhetoric to seriousness at once extends and modifies the traditional opposition between rhetoric and logic, it does not supersede it, and it creates difficulties of its own without eliminating those of the traditional opposition. The attempt to promote rhetoric confronts notorious obstacles, some of which are anticipated in the elementary formulations of Newton Garver in his preface to *Speech and Phenomena:*

> In traditional terms, the central issue of philosophy of language . . . is the issue about the relation of logic and rhetoric. Grammar, having to do with the good order of signs, and their relation to one another, is relatively superficial. Logic and rhetoric, on the other hand, both lead us into more profound areas because they both have to do with the use and interpretation of signs . . . which leads us immediately into the all-important question of their relative priority: can there be two independent foundations of our theory of meaning? Must there be two irreconcilable criteria for the use and interpretation of signs, and hence for linguistic description? Or is one of these two seemingly fundamental disciplines in fact contained in or derivative from the other? When we are able to resolve this fundamental question about the relation of logic to rhetoric, we will then have established a solid vantage point from which to resolve subsidiary questions.[11]

Lanham's solution is to settle all the outstanding questions by begging them. Within an idealized Western order of things, the two principles oscillate without apparent cause or consequence, except that in doing so they maintain an exemplary balance. (The static balance of New Critical ambiguity thus becomes a dynamic oscillation of opposing principles.)

If the traditional opposition between logic and rhetoric has never entirely been superseded within the field of Renaissance studies, it is partly because it is fundamental to the intellectual life of the period under investigation, and because rhetoric emerges in a privileged position in humanist education. It is also, however, an opposition that has been revitalized and regrounded in deconstructive criticism, not without consequences for the study of Renaissance literature.

Derrida envisages, in place of any balanced oscillation of opposing principles, a fixed logocentric structure as constitutive of an all-encompassing (Western) "metaphysics of presence." He characterizes that logocentrism, always already threatened from the margin in the name of rhetoric, not merely as a structure of thought but of power, one maintained by systematic displacement, projection, and repression.[12] Logocentrism, then, exists for us not only as an object of reflection but also as the structure within which we reflect, and which "thinks" us step by step unless we exercise a certain limited power to problematize it. The methodological implications of this position are complex and radical (we are required continuously to maintain a double alertness and to discover resources for thinking the unthinkable), but one immediate consequence of the deconstructive critique is to turn us back on our own reading. How do we read "logocentrically"? How is it possible to read otherwise?

In a sense this reflexive movement has already been initiated, especially in the work of Stanley Fish, who has consistently thematized reading. Yet Fish is the reverse of a deconstructive reader; he has overwhelmingly reaffirmed the logocentrism of major English literature of the seventeenth century, and he has made no bones about his own commitment to a logocentric and even specifically Platonic position.[13] Taking the full consequences of such a position, Fish becomes a resolutely antiaesthetic reader. His "appreciation" of the text requires, if not its actual annihilation, then at least a "self-consuming" action in which aesthetic values and effects are progressively undone until the bare truth prevails *within* the text:

> In the prose of Donne and Milton, and the poetry of Herbert, the stylistic effects—the dislocations, ambiguities, confusions of tenses—

are in the service of the commonplaces of Christian belief. In the *Religio Medici* the commonplaces of Christian belief are in the service of *a succession of stylistic effects,* and our attention is continually diverted from the implications . . . of Browne's statements to the skill he displays in making them. [emphasis added] [14]

Ideally, meaning, even "commonplace" meaning, dominates the text, while "effects" are legitimately held in subservience and deprived of any constitutive status. Thomas Browne transgresses by ostensibly reversing priorities and reducing the commonplaces—themes?—of Christian discourse to the status of red herrings. That is not all:

These, then, are the characteristics of what I have called the aesthetic of the good physician (actually an anti-aesthetic) and on every point Browne stands on the opposite side. He draws attention not *away* from, but *to* himself; his words are not seeds spending their lives in salutary and self-consuming effects, but *objects,* frozen into *rhetorical patterns* which reflect on the *virtuosity* of their author. . . . In terms of the tradition which is at once the subject *and the author* of this book, he is the bad physician. [P. 273; emphasis added]

If there had been no Thomas Browne he would surely have been invented, if only to allow the "anti-aesthetic" its moment of ritual self-affirmation. The "central" tradition is above all, and by definition, *not* rhetorical; within it there can be no division between word and thing, signifier and signified. [15] Words must cease to exist, in the given example, as alien objects and must unselfishly merge into organic Nature, participating in its benign order.

Mere exhibitionism and wordplay are projected into the writing of such a marginal figure as Thomas Browne. In order to maintain a *central* absence of wordplay, however, it is necessary to conserve the opposition between margin and center, which means that "rhetoric" must be conserved, albeit in a marginal or inferior position. The relation between the bad and the good physician, then, will not be parasitic so much as symbiotic. At all events, the priority of the good physician can be upheld only in the presence of the bad physician, while the repeated disavowal of the bad physician entails something like bad faith insofar as he remains a necessary evil.

The singularly apologetic tone of Browne's apologists plays into Fish's hands. Even in the act of defending Browne, they betray their allegiance to the structure of thought that condemns him. It is as if the rhetorical, the performative, even the aesthetic as such, can be defended only with a bad conscience—as second-best—and with the help of gestures that instantly betray their own futility.

Such, one may suspect, is the predetermined fate of defenses of rhetoric, at least insofar as such defenses attempt no more than a reversal of priorities. The defense of rhetoric as an opposing and putatively superior *principle* to that of logic is liable to degenerate into transparent bluster or to become a defense of the palpably indefensible—the defense, for example, of irrational excess, of logical incoherence, of narcissistic display, of violence, and of injustice. Such "principles" cannot seriously be defended (though perhaps the praise of folly is another matter), and quasi-ethical justifications of rhetoric tend to wind up in contradiction, scandal, or impotent silence, a recurrent source of irony in the Platonic dialogues.[16]

The *defense* of rhetoric, however, is really beside the point. It is not as a truly autonomous principle that rhetoric exists in its marginal and suppressed relation to logic, but rather as *all* that logic must deny in order to affirm its own privileged being. What this means, in effect, is that the purity of logic is itself at stake; the repeated purgation of a contaminating rhetoric, which can in reality never be purged, remains the gesture by which logic—and by implication the structure of logocentric order—affirms its own integrity. To illustrate the point in the light of examples already given, we might say that in order to establish the absolute theological seriousness and didactic purity of poems by Donne and Milton, it is not enough to argue textually that these poets "overcome" their own rhetoricity and playful ostentation; it is necessary to set up the purportedly antithetical figure of Browne ("rhetoric" personified) in order to establish both by contrast and by a symbolic expulsion of "rhetoric" the essential purity of the favored authors.

The structure in which the good and bad physician are at once superficially opposed and secretly complicit (if not identical) also occurs in *Surprised by Sin*,[17] only in that case the structure is projected into *Paradise Lost*. The role of Thomas Browne is there assigned to Satan, rhetoric personified, while the role of the good physician, subjecting language entirely to the logical exposition of the truth of Christian belief, is played by God. In terms of Fish's argument, the "effects" of the poem are either self-canceling or are authoritatively canceled by the voice of the omniscient narrator; to read the poem, then, means simply to recognize and submit to its overpowering dialectic. Informed by a radical "antiaesthetic" —which in the nature of things can *only* mean a desire for strict logic to prevail—*Paradise Lost* must continuously disavow its richest effects even in the act of producing them. The reader who willfully "appreciates" those effects is both a misreader and a promoter of false values.

That Fish's view of *Paradise Lost* conforms to Milton's design seems highly probable, yet acceptance of the authority of that design is another matter. *Paradise Lost* has notoriously been "misread," and indeed its repeated misreading is what justifies the existence of *Surprised by Sin*. Certain misreadings are no doubt indefensible, entailing as they do a refusal to acknowledge the evidence of Milton's intentions, but other "misreadings" are of a more challenging kind. There is the Blakean "misreading" in which Milton is of the devil's party without knowing it, and in which, by implication, a false consciousness seeks to impose itself upon the poetic as well as the poet. There are also modern "misreadings" that develop the theme of false or insufficient consciousness, in doing so suggesting that the poem remains a paradoxical monument to the triumph of blind or perverse will, despite all and any rationalistic justifications. My own argument, which is in some degree akin to both the foregoing ones, is simply that Milton's attempt to undo the complicity between poetry—even between language—and "false values" can only be accomplished with the help of Satan as universal scapegoat. The purge cannot be effected with clean hands.

In a sense it is meaningless to protest against the "injustice" or "bad faith" entailed in Milton's employment of a scapegoat device, just as, if one takes at all seriously the conception of an all-encompassing Western "metaphysics of presence," it is meaningless to protest against the injustice of a logocentric structure of thought and value. There will simply be no "Western" alternative, millenarian fantasies notwithstanding.[18] Once this structure is seen to be problematical, however, the possibility arises of a certain critical distance and of play within it. ("Play" in the sense of "being playful" and in the sense of there being some play within the mechanism; "play," too, in the theatrical sense that, once admitted, will confer a degree of legitimacy upon "mere" performativeness.) Recognition of an ineradicable duplicity and bad faith within the very structure of logocentric value is sufficient to reduce the totalitarian hold of that structure upon the mind; it is sufficient also to remove the justification for an unyielding puritanical rigor in the realm not only of morals but also of language. The relentless pursuit of a language purged of effects ceases to be self-justifying, while the superiority of "figures of thought" to "figures of speech" is diminished if not wholly eliminated. The ideal reader ceases to be the one least susceptible to the seductive appeal of the text. If this loss of rigor, "purity," and consistency is conceived to be an unconscionable lapse, it is nevertheless the lapse that "enables" Shakespeare; it is also the lapse that admits a certain leavening of consciousness and wit into the tyrannical realm of the will.

To counterpoise Shakespeare to Milton in this way is not to imply that their respective "positions" are unconditionally available; theirs are positions conditioned by a complex history. A survey of the phase of English literary history that opens (approximately) with the appearance of the Tudor poets, and closes with Milton, will show an initial tolerance of play and "effect" followed by a progressive reduction—an heroic imposition of control—that culminates in the awesome discipline of *Paradise Lost*. To put the case as uncontentiously as possible, critics have found it convenient to approach the literature of the early English Renaissance through models of play (theatrical play, rhetorical performance, festivity, *sprezzatura*, praise of folly), while the same has not applied equally to the later, primarily devotional, works of the seventeenth century. On another level, the reduction of play is evident in the Puritan opposition to the theaters and popular entertainments.[19]

Even allowing for this history, however, which neither Shakespeare nor Milton transcends, a good deal remains at stake in their respective claims to primacy within the English literary tradition. Although there may, in T. S. Eliot's words, be "no competition" between poets, it is not *critically* feasible to have it both ways; a criticism fully capable of assimilating Milton and of identifying itself with his antiaesthetic, rationalistic rigor will be incapable of assimilating Shakespeare, let alone of identifying itself with his metaphoric fluidity, "negative capability," and relativism. Despite Shakespeare's continuing nominal preeminence within the English tradition, the basis of that preeminence has defied adequate theoretical formulation in recent criticism, while Milton has been exemplary for the major criticism of the past decade.

This is not a state of affairs that necessarily calls for a remedy, yet signs of a change have appeared. Particularly under the mediating influence of Derrida, concepts of limitless play, of the primacy of metaphor, of the metaphysics of gender differences, and of a self-sustaining theatricality have reopened the possibility of a general or canonical Shakespeare criticism. In other words, the philosophical prolegomena to such a criticism may have been written, to what ultimate effect it remains to be seen.[20]

It is in this larger context that Nashe acquires a degree of critical importance. First, the critical concepts that promote an understanding of Nashe may also lend themselves to a critical reopening of the question of Shakespeare. Particularly at the level of language, rather than that of form, the study of Nashe contributes to an understanding of Shakespeare, if for no other reason than that the two authors are linked both chronologically and by a common and acknowledged linguistic virtuosity.[21] Second, Nashe's perceived inflation of the "values" of rhetoric, of performance, of verbal excess, and of play calls attention not to the mere existence, but to the problematic nature, of similar "values" in Shakespeare. A third and related point is that, in the course of his career, Nashe generates various rationalizations to accommodate his own practice, and in doing so he may bring to light a similar process in the work of Shakespeare. For all these reasons, a study of Nashe may be a step toward the criticism of Shakespeare, although that is not the whole point. What is closer to being the whole point is the issue of "rhetoric"; a difficult general issue, no doubt, but one that, through the work of Nashe, I wish to consider in a limited frame. If the word "rhetoric" tends to remain in quotes, that is because of the multiplicity of its denotations and connotations, a multiplicity that, for highly pertinent reasons, cannot be reduced to unity. It is part of the very meaning of "rhetoric" in its philosophically extended sense that it embodies a baneful multiplicity, while the protean figure of the rhetorician implies a shifty opportunism, devoid of any ruling principle. The "meaning" of this troubling and complex figure is what I shall now attempt to trace in Nashe criticism.

"Pure" literature; sound without sense, style without substance; unmotivated play. Such are the paradoxical conceptions that repeatedly surface in discussions of Nashe. The idea that Nashe cannot be approached except through the categories of rhetoric or style arises partly from his own insistent prompting, and partly from readers' inability to account in any other way for his hold on the mind. *Theme, message, content,* even *form* rapidly eliminate themselves as critically pertinent terms, and, in this extreme case, *style* becomes not merely the antithesis of *content*, but that which fully discloses itself in the absence of content. Such a concept of style-by-default will be difficult to delimit rigorously, since it will have to accommodate all that remains after the deduction of content, but it is nevertheless one of the avatars of "rhetoric" that cannot be reduced to simple definition. It can, however, be characterized up to a point in historical and technical terms.

One immediate result of Nashe's characterization as a stylist has been extensive and often fruitful analysis of his prose.[22] In such discussions—stylistic analysis properly speaking—oppositions between Form and Content or between Norm and Deviation are legitimately taken for granted in order to faciltate technical analysis. In effect, the primary oppositions on which any concept of style must depend are placed out of contention in the interests of neutral analysis. Even if this sanitizing procedure more fully reflects the will to purity than the accomplished fact, neither the justification nor the results of stylistic analysis are now in question. It is the metaphysics rather than the mechanics of style that concern me here.

In his introduction to his own edition of *The Unfortunate Traveller*, John Berryman challenges the repeated claim that Nashe survives purely as a stylist.[23] Berryman argues that style is never enough in itself to guarantee literary survival and that Nashe's style is in any case erratic; it may be distinguished, but not to the ineffable degree that Nashe's apologists seem to require. Well qualified to judge, and acting under no compulsion to detect "style" in every crevice of Nashe's work, Berryman can be both particular and discriminating:

> Suppose we begin with an example. To Surrey's long discourse of his love for Geraldine, Jack responds mentally in the narrative as follows:
>> Not a little was I delighted with this unexpected love storie, especially from a mouth out of which was nought wont to march but sterne precepts of grauetie & modestie. I swear unto you I thought his companie the better by a thousand crownes, because he had discarded those nice tearmes of chastitie and continencie. Now I beseech God love me so well as I love a plaine dealing man: earth is earth, flesh is flesh, earth will to earth, and flesh unto flesh: fraile earth, fraile flesh, who can keepe you from the work of your creation?
>
> I have taken, on consideration, a passage which no one would be likely to overpraise or hold commonplace, a suggestive but median passage, though exalted in the close.
>
> A spectrum of points, not exhaustive: The word order of the first sentence is unremarkable, yet reminds me that Nashe is (I hope I do not exaggerate) one of the masters of English prose. Inversion or rearrangement for rhythm, emphasis, and simulation of the (improved) colloquial . . . rapid, offhand, natural, the order is still highly periodic. Note then how physical it is ("from a mouth") and how active ("march"): major notes of the style. It is a self-conscious style, but *alert*, not laboured. . . .
>
> Impromptu and searching, Nashe's prose often seems, not a *first* anything, but a last high achievement of the impromptu and searching vigor exemplified in Tyndale's Bible (1525). [Pp. 11–12]

This passage might be read as a salutary demystification of Nashe's style, one that discloses its concrete features, its historical relativity, and its conditioning by forces beyond individual control. Berryman accounts for Nashe's appeal by saying that he writes well enough, but is also sufficiently imaginative and self-dramatizing to engage our interest. What is the problem?

On the point of answering that there is none, we may detect Berryman relapsing into a notion of purity. After imputing to Nashe an overriding concern with "the medium, with prose itself" (p. 17), Berryman asserts that "as a novelist . . . he cannot much attract us, but his claim as a *writer* is permanent" (p. 18). Still denying that matters are quite so simple, Berryman finds himself placing Nashe with the help of a distinction Coleridge applied to the visual arts:

> The beautiful in the object may be referred to two elements—lines and colours; the first belonging to the shapely (*forma, formalis, formosus*) and in this to the law and the reason; the second to the lively, the free, the spontaneous and the self-justifying.[24]

In effect, if not in all pedantic literalness, Nashe represents pure color, which being translated from the realm of pigment into that of language, means pure rhetoric (*color, coloratus*). This color will also, in terms of the given antithesis, imply pure irrationality, lawlessness—and perhaps "beauty."

Berryman, like so many others, appears unable to sustain a moderate, pluralistic view of Nashe, and slowly comes round to the position he begins by challenging. Although Berryman's analysis is neither extensive nor technically ambitious, there is nothing to suggest that further practical criticism would lead to a different conclusion and, without Berryman's tact, such analysis may lapse into bathos:

> Most of the sentences begin with nouns or pronouns; but the first, third, and next to last begin with another part of speech. Toward the middle of the paragraph there is a long sentence, followed by a fairly short and then a very short sentence . . . the total effect—with the hard "c" and explosive "p" sounds . . . is a more dynamic style than Lyly's.[25]

All of which goes to prove that Nashe engages us primarily as a stylist.

The effect of Berryman's discussion is at once to reinstate the sharpest possible distinction between style and content, thus supplying Nashe with the transcendental justification of stylistic purity, and to leave behind many unanswered questions. If Nashe's style is both impromptu and erratic, to what extent does mastery imply a high degree of control? Is it ever possible to distinguish between the sublime and the careless effect? To what extent does Nashe's style reflect aesthetic choice or simply the inertia he is unable to overcome? Can the "effectiveness" of writing be assessed wholly without reference to its ends? To ask such questions is to suggest Berryman's reversion to an aesthetic mysticism in which style becomes the saving grace or transcendental essence of writing. In asserting the absolute privilege of style, an assertion underlined by his purely stylistic characterization of Tyndale's Bible, Berryman succumbs to an inverted logocentrism, that of *oratio* rather than *ratio*, both of which terms ambivalently inhabit the single term *logos*.

The drastic antithesis between style and content that Berryman invokes is, of course, not limited to Berryman's criticism or to discussions of Nashe. On the contrary, it has appeared regularly in discussions of Tudor prose, and many of Nashe's near-contemporaries have also, at one time or another, been characterized as pure stylists. In fact, it has been virtually normal practice to approach the prose writing of the period 1575–1600 through categories of style or rhetoric, and to define the achievement of particular writers in stylistic or rhetorical terms (euphuism, the "scrollwork" of Sidney, Hooker's "massive sonorities," and so forth).[26] Yet in one pertinent case this dualism has been challenged, and moreover in a way that appears finally to lay the ghost of pure style. Jonas Barish, refuting the received idea that Lyly's style is purely ornamental, argues powerfully that "antithesis, habitual and even obsessive as it is in Lyly's thought, may be regarded as simply one aspect of a more comprehensive stylistic phenomenon, logicality . . . the style of *Euphues* offers for our inspection the world as antithesis."[27] Barish does not simply reverse his predecessors' arguments, promoting style at the expense of content, but tries to eliminate this dualism entirely. Logicality becomes, without apparent contradiction, a stylistic effect. Under these circumstances, the entire issue of "rhetoric" disappears.

Barish's monism undoubtedly marks an advance on his predecessors' crude dualism, but the monist reduction is finally illusory:

> This distinction, which drives a wedge between style and content, and
> treats them as though they enjoyed a separate and independent exis-
> tence, if it interferes with objective descriptions of style, interferes still
> more with any effort to get at the heart of a writer's artistic universe,
> where style and meaning interpenetrate. [Pp. 15–16]

The phemenon of interpenetration is itself strictly mystical, and
the very description in which it occurs embodies familiar divisions
between presence and absence, center and periphery, organism and
mechanism. Interpenetration is not universal, but takes place only
at the heart of things, and this fusion does not preclude the survival,
even if in paradoxical form, of a terminology of style and content.

In reality, Barish's achievement is somewhat other than his own
manifesto would suggest. Instead of healing the split between ornamental figures and meaningful words, he assigns a semantic role to
syntax and thus in one stroke transforms a pure rhetorical excess
(or redundancy) into a pure economy of representation. The
"world," even if it is only that of the artist, becomes that which is
signified by a given syntactical order, and any apparent lack of
significance in Lyly's mechanical euphuism is more than adequately
redressed. This success is paid for, however, by the transformation
of reading into a Sisyphean allegorization of syntax.

Apart from any inherent questionableness in Barish's approach,
his argument (more strictly, his proposal of a way of reading) lacks
general applicability and cannot thus account for the phenomenon
represented by Nashe or by Renaissance prose in general. Only in
the conspicuous special case does syntax assume its greatest significance. It is at once the strength and limitation of Barish's work
that it centers itself on writers who attend obsessively to syntactic
patterning and control, and who even face one another as repre-
sentatives of opposing syntactic dogmas (Lyly versus Jonson). If
these writers present "a world for our inspection," it is perhaps a
psychological world in which a relentlessly systematic will prevails,
generating prose that is both eccentric and notoriously unreadable.
By contrast, in the prose of Shakespeare, which is undeniably

readable, Barish shows that a Lylyan structure of balance and antithesis is present but not overriding; there is within that prose a principle of order but not one that gains a mechanical ascendancy. (Similarly, if there is an element of Jonsonian disorder in Shakespeare's prose, it too does not gain absolute ascendancy. Perhaps the point to be made is that syntax that fully yields "a world for our inspection" is liable to be self-defeatingly programmatic, a possibility to be borne in mind in the next phase of my argument.)

It would appear, then, that the issue with which I began remains open to consideration and that the phenomenon of an unreduced excess of "rhetoric" may still need to be explored. That phenomenon, too, can continue to be represented under the name of Nashe. Or so it seems until that possibility is challenged head on, as it is by Rosemond Tuve, who in turn calls on Gabriel Harvey to testify:

> No school advocated as desirable poetic imagery "that naturall stile" for which Harvey taunts Nashe so unmercifully. Harvey's snorts of ironic scorn for him who calls carelessness "nature" show how far both he and his enemies were from a poetic in which "spontaneous" meant praise for the artist:
>
>> It is for Cheeke or Ascham to stand levelling of Colons, or squaring of Periods, by measure and number: his [Nashe's] penne is like a spigot, and the Wine presse is a dullard to his Ink-presse. There is a certain lively and frisking thing ... that scorneth to be a bookeworme, or to imitate the excellentest artificiality of the most renowned worke-masters that antiquity affourdeth. The witt of this & that odd Modernist [sic] is their owne ... Whuist Art! And Nature aduance thy precious Selfe in thy most gorgeous and magnificent robes.
>
> Those who substituted vigor for art continued to be laughed at. The "terrible gunpowder" of the pamphlet style did not find adherents in any poetic school; and what is analogous, in imagery, to "squaring the periods" in sentence structure continued to characterize all but ballad wits.[28]

Simply for the record, let us recall that Nashe's prose is not governed by a poetic, but rather, as *The Unfortunate Traveller* suggests, by an antipoetic (which seeks to establish the domain of "prose as prose"), and that his poetry is of an exemplary squareness. The decorum of his prose, moreover, is unassailably learned rather than vulgar, and his work never less than a popular art.[29]

The real question raised by both Tuve and Harvey concerns Nashe's alleged incompetence. His pretensions to a sublime freedom, naturalness, or saving spontaneity are dismissed, and along with them the possibility of style as a transcendent or natural grace. Capitalizing on a carelessness that even such an apologist as Berryman concedes, and that is hardly redeemed by Nashe's alternate special-pleading for an aesthetic of spontaneity and self-exculpation as a victim of economic pressure, Tuve and Harvey collapse any possible distinction between style and rhetoric, reinstating the primacy of strict decorum. More accurately, they assimilate style into rhetoric, identifying it with conformity rather than deviation, immanence rather than transcendence.

Although theme or content cease to be important under this scheme of things, rhetoric does not accordingly emerge in any elemental guise, but becomes equivalent to good form. Instead of standing in baffling opposition to logical understanding or ethical principle, rhetoric stands for order, knowledge, and cultivation. Any power, intellectual anarchism, or free play is denied to style, which becomes the very sign of civilization as opposed to elemental vigor. In attempting to assert himself against an ideal order of things, Nashe not only becomes a comic outlaw figure (a role Nashe espouses on occasion), but Tuve and Harvey undertake the vindication of the law.

The extent to which the strictures of Tuve in particular are based on sheer error makes a detailed rebuttal unnecessary. What is unexpected is that the problem Nashe presents can evidently be felt from the side of rhetoric as well as that of logic. The idealization of pure form (geometrically squared periods) is, however, a logocentrism under another and lesser name, a fact that speedily eliminates any apparent paradox in the "pure" stylists' being assailed from the side of style. Tuve's sublimation of rhetoric into a poetic, together with her prescription of a fully and mathematically rationalized language, represents precisely the kind of attempt we have previously seen to reduce a threatening linguistic excess and to reinstate an ideal economy of language, albeit in a social rather than a metaphysical frame of reference ("good form").

What is also apparent in the arguments of both Tuve and Harvey is the paradox of the cricket and the serpent. Ostensibly, Nashe's outlaw performance exposed him only to derision, yet after the lapse of four centuries he must be exposed to further cutting derision; he found no adherents, but must be prevented again from exerting any influence. His self-evidently futile opposition to right reason and authority must nevertheless be exposed as pernicious and crushed under the weight of authority. Tuve and Harvey's assault on Nashe is, in short, self-contradictory, and in Tuve's case that assault is accompanied by a significant omission. If there is one thing that everybody knows, it is that Harvey, not Nashe, was made to look foolish—even tragically absurd—in the two authors' prolonged war of words. What is being denied, and thus unintentionally reaffirmed, is the irreducible power and opportunistic success of Nashe's rhetoric. This denial of Nashe's power is linked also to an attempt to immobilize him as a self-defeatingly committed modernist-naturalist-vitalist, whereas the protean quality of Nashe's writing (and "position") is what enables it to elude easy capture.

It could be argued that Nashe is more sensitive to stylistic decorum and to the meaning of various stylistic gestures than to anything else.[30] It could also be argued that the naturalness Tuve and Harvey disavow is more consistent with Renaissance rhetorical theory than is the strict decorum they prescribe. One could easily invoke the term *sprezzatura* in this context; one could also point out that rigid prescriptions are, in Elizabethan rhetorical theory, insufficient to guarantee a true decorum. Such decorum can, according to George Puttenham, take virtually any form depending upon the context; ideal decorum also lies finally beyond the power of art or of specification:

> In all things to vse decencie, it is onely that giueth euery thing his good grace & without which nothing in mans speach could seeme good or gracious, in so much as manie times it makes a bewtifull figure fall into deformitie, and on th'other side a vicious speach seeme pleasaunt and bewtiful: this decencie is therefore the line & leuell of all good makers

to do their busines by. But herein resteth the difficultie, to know what
this good grace is, & wherein it consisteth, for peraduenture it be easier
to conceaue then to expresse. . . . The Greekes call this good grace of
euery thing in his kinde, τό πσέπου, the Latines [*decorum*] ; we in oure
vulgar call it by a scholasticall terme [*decencie*] ; our owne Saxon English term is [seemlynesse] . . . we call it also [*comelynesse*] . . . [*pleasant approche*] [31]

Finally, Puttenham can only exemplify, in a series of anecdotes,
the mysterious thing that passes under many names.

It would be possible to extend these arguments, but to do so
here would be superfluous. What I have sought to establish, using
Nashe as the case in point, is the phenomenon, reaffirmed by a
succession of readers, of a linguistic excess surpassing any func-
tional explanation, any acceptable rationale, or any power of repression. The persistence of this excess, which I have identified not
with so-called natural language but with the conscious play and
manipulation of "rhetoric," [32] allows on one hand for reading as an
act of aesthetic appreciation (not always this side of idolatory)
and on the other for reading as the attempted reduction of an of-
fensive superfluity. In general, I would suggest, reading implies the
latter in the criticism I have considered. It has not been my purpose to reverse this trend, but rather in some degree to deconstruct
these fixed alternatives before proceeding.

CHAPTER 2

THE LOSS
OF DECORUM

The critics whose work I surveyed in the previous chapter are linked in a common effort to produce what is by implication lacking in the literature of the English Renaissance, namely a language of final order and ultimate significance. It goes almost without saying that their effort parallels and repeats that of authors within the period, especially Puritan ones. The existence of such a language would imply, among other things, the final elimination of the rhetorical persona with his particular self-interest and repertoire of effects; the reduction of wordplay and linguistic duplicity; the apotheosis of the impersonal theme; and the substitution of a sufficient and authoritative speech for a mere power of words. Within a "fallen" world, the achievement of such a language would necessarily entail a reversal or overcoming of the status quo. The author is always situated within a language already misappropriated, duplicitous, and subject to rhetorical exploitation; it is from within that the restorative project must be planned and executed.

There is of course no major writer of the English Renaissance unskilled in the techniques of rhetorical expression and wordplay, since those are skills that constitute the *sine qua non* for a literary career within the period. Probably because of this, and because of the accompanying rhetorical self-consciousness, there is also no major writer of the period who does not participate in the dream of healing and restoration, or seek the ultimate triumph in language of the erected wit over the infected will. There are, however, significant differences of degree in the psychological sophistication and single-mindedness with which various authors translate such dreams into programs. Puritan rationalism and antitheatricalism are not universally conceived to be restorative, while the mere cultural presence of rhetoric and theatricality (even of the physical theater) "postpones" and renders infinitely problematical the desired outcome.[1]

In saying this I have, of course, assimilated theatricality to "rhetoric" and have also by implication introduced the topic of relativistic dramatic form as opposed (say) to absolutist epic form. While there is a clearly established continuity in the period between rhetorical performance and debate on one hand, and theater on the other,[2] this extension of the field of "rhetoric" to incorporate drama exceeds the scope of my argument. Reverting to a narrower frame, I will suggest that for Nashe, but not for him alone, the values and motives of performance are to be acknowledged rather than denied. The *logical* contingency or egregiousness of such bastard values and motives does not do away with them, if for no other reason than that they are so deep-rooted in the divided ("fallen") mind.[3] They are there to be lived with. Moreover, they are powerful enough to generate the hypothesis of an entire antiworld in which they prevail, an antiworld of which "rhetoric" becomes, paradoxically, the signifier.

To characterize this antiworld, it might seem sufficient to speak of the world as opposed to the spirit, taking the world to encompass the full range of traditional pejoratives associated with worldliness, political manipulation, and sophisticated savoir-faire, yet something more than this is required. What has to be conceived—what a demonic rhetoric allows to be conceived—is a world of negative energy, of perpetually inverted or subverted order, uninformed by any redeeming principle. Such a world will be characterized not by its conformity to the cynical commonplaces of experience, but rather by its violent negativity, by its progressive deformation or transformation in the absence of any sustaining structure or ideal principle. To conceive of an antiworld is, in short, to conceive of a world in which an interminable undoing or disruption of good order becomes at once the condition of existence and the source of power. Such an antiworld is not to be characterized by any mere dualism of Good and Evil or even by its own material antagonism to the ideal, but by its simultaneous antagonism to and parasitism upon an absent ideal.[4] Such is the world of which rhetorical excesses speak, and in which the egregious motives and values of performance prevail.

I have already suggested that the defense of rhetoric relies upon untenable paradoxes and melodramatic reversals; I would now add that a serious world view or philosophy implied by any such defense is equally untenable and melodramatic. The example of Gorgias remains cautionary in this regard.[5] The mere cultural presence of rhetoric, however, together with the specter it evokes of an antiworld, is another matter. Rhetoric's simply being there and exerting a continuous force is enough to induce, if not a conviction of its primacy, then at least a profound irresolution about the nature of "reality." While performance retains its elemental and sometimes shocking force, it forestalls the triumph of univocal or rational order.

Such is the state of affairs revealed in the work of Nashe. Without committing himself uneqivocally to performance as an absolute value or to the systematic promulgation of an antiworld, the ongoing possibilities of "rhetoric" are extensively explored in his work.

Nashe begins his career by identifying himself explicitly with the dogmas and values enshrined in Ascham's *The Schoolmaster*. His doing so identifies him with a conservative, anti-Ramist position in Tudor humanism;[6] it also commits him to the assumption that a good order of language is both the sign and the origin of a good order within the world and within the individual mind. The achievement of this good order by an English writer depends to a high degree on classical imitation and translation (following the best Latin models and assuming the "character" thus constituted); it depends to a lesser degree upon recognition of the genius of particular languages, since failure of such recognition results in bastardization and a supplanting of what is proper (legitimate, inherent) by artificial novelties. Ascham writes:

> For marke all aiges: looke vpon the whole course of both the Greeke and Latin tonge, and ye shall surelie finde, that, whan apte and good wordes began to be neglected, and the properties of those two tonges to be confounded, than also began ill deedes to spring: strange maners to oppresse good orders, newe and fond opinions to striue with olde and trewe doctrine.[7]

The reconciliation of an intuited linguistic propriety with the necessity of imitating exotic models continues to be perceived as a major challenge to English authors right up to the twentieth century. Ascham's own educational program of translation to and fro between Latin and English is designed to satisfy the requirements both of propriety and of imitation, yet the loss of linguistic virtue—the production of synthetic or merely novel effects—becomes a significant critical issue, both in Nashe's period and in Nashe's own career.[8] It is indicative of Ascham's profound conservatism, however, that he defines innovation in entirely negative terms, while the process of linguistic *change* remains conceivable only as a series of historical catastrophes. Ideally, language(s) would remain fixed in their moments of classical perfection, yet this possibility appears always to be denied by a malign historical necessity ("marke all aiges"). This linguistic idealism, to the service of which Ascham's rhetorical program is subordinated, remains a point of reference throughout Nashe's career.

Nashe's admiration for Ascham and his allegiance to Ascham's "school" are enthusiastically proclaimed in *The Anatomy of Absurdity,* yet even in that early work, which virtually becomes a parodic treatise on good order, the impossibility of embodying Ascham's conceptions—at least outside the schoolroom—is finally acknowledged; the speaker of the *Anatomy* can in the end only refer the reader to Ascham, particularly his *Schoolmaster,* for the enlightenment that the *Anatomy* cannot give. It is, however, against the background of this early admiration for Ascham, this conservative valuation of propriety and hostility to innovation, and perhaps above all this intense mythologization of language that

Nashe's career as virtuoso, innovator, and scandalous wit unfolds. Without ever forswearing his early commitments, Nashe embarks on an increasingly—even tormentedly—paradoxical career, yet one in which the priority of language as well as the limitless significance of linguistic order (or anarchy) continue to be reasserted. No doubt it might be said that Nashe succumbs to history (the history Ascham seeks to forestall); no doubt Nashe too, in common with many of his peers, must embrace the risks of rhetorical impropriety and linguistic innovation in order to pursue a career under the peculiar conditions of the 1590s, yet Nashe's "schooling" ensures that none of this can occur without acute consciousness, deliberate experimentation, and frequent reappraisal. Moreover, Nashe (willingly or not) reveals the stresses that Ascham attempts to minimize or eliminate.

The pursuit of an ideal decorum, a process that invests "rhetoric" with its only admissible logic and ethical justification, is in difficulties from the start. Any attempt within a purely technical and pedagogic framework to achieve a good order of words must fall short, since such an order is ultimately unthinkable without transcendental foundation, a deficiency Ascham himself appears to acknowledge when he writes that without "the trewe doctrine of Gods holie Bible," the learning and example of the ancients are "fine edge tooles in a fole or a mad mans hand" (p. 266). Moreover, imitation of rhetorical models is not exempt from the strictures laid upon imitation per se, which Ascham seems to acknowledge by default when he writes that "of this *Imitation* writeth Plato at large in 3 *de Rep,* but it doth not moch belong at this time to our purpose" (p. 266). Although "3 *de Rep*" does not embody Plato's principal arguments on the deficiencies of imitation, it announces the problem, and it also begins to discount the pedagogic value of rhetorical schooling, bound as that practice is to performance rather than knowledge, self-dramatization rather than self-formation.

In addition to the theoretical obstacles to the achievement of "good order"—a good order that could at best be academic only—there are practical obstacles. In his particular historical situation, Nashe implicitly asks what degree of order is compatible with economic pressure, with the established requirements of disorderly readers, and with the exigencies of the commercial press.[9] These practical issues cannot be set aside in any discussion of Nashe, since he makes them vociferously his own. The preemptive power of contingency becomes one of his standing grievances. What is capable of being written can never be more than an indication of what might have been written under favorable circumstances; accordingly, the written work can only mark the absence of the ideal work, at the same time conferring on itself the status of a mere advertisement or a show of force.

Nashe embarrassingly, so to speak, insists on the preemptive power of contingency, at the same time revealing the ascendancy of mercenary disorder over ideal order. Embarrassment arises from that fact that the absence of an ideal decorum, as well as the absence of a full determining power over language, is so starkly exposed. Furthermore, the inadmissible connection between "rhetoric" and material gain—the connection that traditionally defines the sophist—is not denied but repeatedly advertised, to the detriment of any possibility of good order. Hence, no doubt, some of the resentment Nashe arouses.

If Nashe does not just accept the fate of the hack, that is because he asserts within his own world of contingency a certain residual power of authorship—a power that is never sufficient to its own ideal ends, but persists even in its own deformity and deflection. On one occasion, too, which I shall discuss, Nashe seemingly attempts a total recovery of language from within a debased popular form, in doing so accomplishing grand parody rather than grand style.[10] Before proceeding to these large issues, however, I wish to pause over some formative episodes in Nashe's early career, attempting in some degree to concretize the notion of "rhetoric" that applies to his work. I shall also (unnecessarily for many readers) review the familiar history of Nashe's emergence as a stylist. The moments I have selected for review are mainly ones in which Nashe, while shrinking from the unthinkably naive repudiation of all decorum, nevertheless renders decorum suspect or problematical.

At the beginning of his own public career, Nashe writes a preface to Robert Greene's *Menaphon* (1589), in which he at once distances himself from Greene's performance, establishes his own priorities, and reveals an overriding preoccupation with matters of style. His characterization of Greene's work, in which he disregards the fact that *Menaphon* is a narrative romance in prose rather than an oration, is purely stylistic:

> I come (sweet friend) to thy *Arcadian Menaphon,* whose attire (though not so stately, yet comely) doth intitle thee aboue all other to that *temperatum dicendi genus* which *Tully* in his Orator termeth true eloquence.[11]

The content of the work remains entirely nominal, or becomes reduced to an Arcadian essence, while style occupies the foreground, becoming the substance of Greene's achievement as well as the true product of rhetorical imitation. If ideal decorum is maintained, it is also separated from any essential virtue and need not correspond to (or express) a determining inner condition. True eloquence paradoxically becomes a form of attire, sufficient unto itself and released from any further obligation.

While Nashe may thus seem at the outset of his career to legitimize pure style, he also fatefully commits himself to the metaphor of style-as-garb, and in doing so reinscribes within his own work the opposition between inner and outer. In identifying stylistic decorum with outward conformity rather than with a profound fitness of things, Nashe establishes the possibility that such decorum is essentially hollow or that outward appearances may be meaningless, contradictory, or treacherous. Even a perfect correspondence between appearance and essence may reveal negative characteristics, as we shall see, while the mere existence of stylistic garb may seem to establish its own logical and interpretive requirements. On the other hand, the release of style from any ontological or epistemological anchorage (its trivialization in that sense) makes it available for manipulation or refashioning.

Having once introduced the clothes metaphor, Nashe can (or must) play out its implications. His attempts to transform a modest decorum of style by amplification, extravagance, and violence—all of which are recognized characteristics of Nashe's various performances—appear in the early phase of his career to confront him all the more relentlessly with the deficiency of content or, if not that, with the correspondence between a flashy style and a "feminine" vanity that compulsively "a-dresses" itself. (This definitive pun belongs to Nashe, as does the diagnosis.)[12] The one character seemingly implied by (we might say constituted by) a departure from modest decorum is that of Pride, of whose reign self-advertising style becomes a perpetual allegory.

In introducing Greene, then, Nashe casually introduces a metaphor to the full implications of which his own career becomes an extended testimony. Without ever developing this metaphor to the absurdly logical conclusion of a Swiftian clothes-philosophy (in which the universe is constituted *as* clothing in a final turnabout), Nashe is threatened with victimization by it, and with the corresponding necessity of a "saving" violence, extravagance, or ingenuity. In the short term, however, Nashe attempts in the *Menaphon* preface to reconstitute style as a form of (self-) expression rather than of outward conformity, of power rather than of "sweetness." The style of the preface is an early instance of the anti-Ciceronianism that Barish has so effectively characterized as performative, unbalanced, and antilogical.[13] To the extent that Nashe practices such a style, he represents an avant-garde; he also establishes some tenuous theoretical positions.

In presenting Greene as a model university wit of the school of Ascham, Nashe extols, as we have seen, an eloquence that conforms to the *temperatum dicendi genus* authorized by "Tully." Greene thus becomes a model of decorum, at the same time justifying the program of rhetorical imitation in which he has been nurtured. Notoriously, however, Nashe damns his "sweet friend" with faint praise and then proceeds to upstage him, revealing a lack of interest in, or commitment to, the values Greene represents. The *felt* lack to which Nashe's preface as a performance draws attention is that of power and self-determination.[14] A merely demure wit remains a puerile figure in the presence of his masters, preeminently "Tully." Imitation, moderation, balance, decency; all are incompatible with the achievement of a power and self-determination for which Nashe's preface becomes an impassioned if unavowed plea. The mere imitation of violent, hyperbolical

28

models offers no solution, however, since such imitations over-shoot the mark and become ineptly bombastic:

> The seruile imitation of vaine glorious Tragedians, who contend not so seriously to excell in action, as to embowell the cloudes in a speech of comparison, thinking themselues then more initiated in Poets immortal-ity, if they but once get *Boreas* by the beard and the heauenly Bull by the deaw-lap. [P. 311]

What then remains? Let us recall Nashe's historically important proposal of an "extemporall" style:

> Giue me the man whose extemporall veine in any humour will excell our greatest Art-maisters deliberate thoughts; whose inuentions, quicker then his eye, will challenge the prowdest Rhetoritian to the contention of like perfection with like expedition. [P. 312]

In enacting a shift from university wit to "humour" as the foun-dation of rhetorical performance, Nashe reestablishes a vital connection between speech and being, substituting an impulsive expressiveness for premeditated effects. He also resituates rhetorical performance in an agonistic rather than a mimetic context, establish-ing it as a mode of competitive play rather than "servile" repeti-tion. Ascham's "doctrine" of imitation is also replaced by a counter-doctrine of antagonism to figures of established rhetorical authority. As figures of ponderous, perhaps hubristic, grandeur, the "Art maisters" and "prowd Rhetoricians" become vulnerable, and they can be overreached in a mode antithetical to their own. This mode, moreover, founds itself on unrepressed "humour," that is to say, on arbitrary excess, self-assertion, or moodiness in the face of reasoned deliberation.[15] To be made in the image of the masters is to lack both self-definition and any inherent principle of vitality, while to oppose these masters is paradoxically to equal and even to excel them.

The achievement of an inventive, self-affirming rhetoric thus depends upon a principle of almost pure wilful antagonism, yet the licensing of "humour" supplies that rhetoric (strictly now an antirhetoric) with an organic basis lacking in mechanical imitation. Such a rhetoric "says nothing" because it *is* the pure expression of the physical-intellectual being who speaks it, and whom it speaks. If the term *decorum* still applies, it can only be the decorum of the given humor in the given moment, an absolutely unfixed decorum. Such a decorum may be a contradiction in terms, but only in such contradictory terms can the liabilities of conventional decorum apparently be overcome.

So far so good. Nashe can apparently supply, *pace* Tuve, the reasons of his unreason, while the pursuit of an inimitable or elemental quality of performance becomes for Nashe a conscious goal at a very early stage in his career. The aggressiveness of Nashe's rhetoric is effectively rationalized and its outlaw character ostensibly kept within the agonistic bounds of regulated contention. It breaches strict decorum only in the name of an irrepressible force that shapes its own decorum. If Nashe's account, together with his practice, awakens traditional suspicions of the unprincipled violence and self-assertiveness of rhetoric, it also opposes the good of humor to the at least questionable value of surface conformity.

What remains to be said is that, in sacrificing rhetorical decorum in one sense, Nashe revives it in another, no longer identifying it with balance, stasis, and moderation, but with fluidity, force, and unpredictability. What might legitimately be designated a romantic rhetoric thus takes the place of a classical rhetoric now rendered effete, but no "escape" from rhetoric or the principle of decorum has been effected. Not only does Nashe not invent his own language, but the desire for a perfectly self-expressive and extemporal style can, despite the implicit self-congratulation, be expressed only in the form of a wish: "Giue me the man whose extemporall veine." The speaker remains, wittingly or not, the prisoner of rhetoric, his barely articulated desire for a new freedom arising more from the consciousness of existing limitations than from any capacity to formulate a positive revolutionary program. Moreover, a vitiating contradiction remains insofar as Nashe wills a transcendence of rhetoric or a new power of self-determination. The continuing parasitism of his own antagonistic mode upon a prior model of rhetorical correctness and upon a prior figure of rhetorical authority (Cicero) makes his own self-emancipation questionable, a state of affairs to which Barish interestingly draws attention in his discussion of anti-Ciceronianism as a general phenomenon.[16] The repetitive violence of the emancipating gesture may merely become the sign of a continuing bondage. We have nevertheless seen that the gesture itself, together with the "presumptuous" claims attending it, are enough to bring down the full weight of repressive ridicule (and "misunderstanding").

In the foregoing paragraphs I have covered some ground wholly familiar to readers of Nashe criticism, attempting little more than a shift in some of the emphases of existing criticism and literary history. My aim has been partly to indicate the theoretical matrix in which Nashe's early works are situated, but also to establish points of reference from which the unfolding of his career becomes intelligible. While I would suggest that the imperatives of the *Menaphon* preface are never entirely superseded in Nashe's work, that work reveals a continuing process of reappraisal in which the nature and power of rhetoric are always at stake.

In his early (anonymous) pamphlet *An Almond for a Parrot* Nashe writes as an enlisted university wit in the pamphlet war between the Anglican episcopacy and the pseudonymous Puritan author Martin Marprelate.[17] This controversy concerned the proper form of church government, with Marprelate representing the presbyterian theory of government by elders, as opposed to the episcopal theory of government by a hierarchy. Marprelate's effectiveness depended partly on his yoking a rhetoric of festive abuse and popular comedy to the serious purposes he sought to accomplish; attempts by the episcopacy to respond in a style of dignified admonition were not only ineffective but virtually ludicrous in the circumstances. Among other university wits, including Lyly, Nashe was called on to respond in kind to the witty, scurrilous, theatrical assaults by Martin Marprelate on episcopal authority in general and on reigning bishops in particular. Prohibited by decorum (and perhaps by incapacity) from replying in kind, Bishops Whitgift and Cooper relied on the talents of the university wits, but also on their own considerable powers of arbitrary arrest, censorship, and torture, to silence Marprelate.[18] Nashe's most solidly attested contribution to this pamphlet war is *Almond* (ca. 1589).

Decorum becomes the principal bone of contention in this

pamphlet. Although Nashe incorporates in the pamphlet the standard episcopal arguments against presbyterian leveling in church
government,[19] what is repeatedly and comically exposed is the
flagrant indecorum of Puritan manners, customs, and language.
The speaker in *Almond* refers, for example, to a pastor who "tom-
bled his wife naked into the earth at high noone, without sheete or
shroude to cover her shame, breathing ouer her in an audible
voice: Naked I came out of my mothers wombe, and naked I shall
return againe" (p. 344). Here propriety demands a decent covering,
while the unceremoniousness of the Puritan burial becomes a
cause of scandalized amusement. Another anecdote in a similar
vein:

> This hors-holy father, preaching on a time in Saint Maries at Oxford,
> came off with this mannerly comparison: There is an vglie and mon-
> strous beast in our tongue called a hogge, and this vgly and monstrous
> beast in boistrous and tempesteous weather lifts vp his snoute into the
> ayre, and cryes wrough, wrough; euen so (deare people) the children of
> God in the troublesome time of temptations cry, Our helpe is in the
> name of the Lord. [P. 373]

Again we see a failure of mannerliness, and one moreover that
bathetically threatens the saving distinctions between man and
beast, the sublime and the ridiculous ("hors-holy father"). Decorum becomes a matter of preserving distinctions, thus maintaining a hierarchical succession by degree from the animal through
the human to the divine.

The effect of Nashe's retailing of such anecdotes is both to "expose" the farcical folly of Puritanism and to reaffirm communal
values of propriety and decorum. To see the joke at the expense of
the Puritans is implicitly to assent to the need for decorum. Where
serious arguments fail, malicious wit becomes the instrument
through which decorum is conserved and a community that "sees
the joke" reconstituted. The effectiveness of the method is affirmed
by Isaac Walton in his "Life of Whitgift":

> [Tom Nashe's] merry Wit made some sport and such a discovery of
> their absurdities as (which is strange) he put a greater stop to these
> Pamphlets than a much wiser man had been able.[20]

The problem that arises with this "method," however, is that reliance on wit may expose the insecurity of the foundations. The very anecdotes Nashe relates are subversive of the decorum they uphold. What Nashe embodies in both anecdotes is not only the huge liberating force of bathos but also the unassailably literal conformity of Puritanism to the divine will. The decent shrouding of a corpse to cover its actual and symbolic nakedness would thwart the divine injunction, while the "hors-holy father's" analogizing of men to pigs in stormy weather is comically deflating and even salutary in its denial of human sufficiency. The ultimate vanity (in every sense) of decorum is betrayed by the very anecdotes that enforce it. Moreover, the Puritan world Nashe displays in *Almond* threatens to become one of utopian indifference, festive vitality,[21] and animal well-being, its innocent comedy constituting a challenge to vain pretension. Nashe's consciousness both of Rabelaisian excess and Erasmian folly heightens the ambivalence of his representation.

Moving in *Almond* in relation to a vertical axis of degree and to a horizontal axis of playful indifference, Nashe cannot finally come to rest. His irresolution is marked by shifts in tone and rhetorical persona throughout *Almond;* at one moment the voice is that of paternal admonition while at another it becomes that of mischievous conspiracy:

Well, come on it what will, Martin and I will allow of no such doinges.
[P. 342]

No fixed decorum or persona emerges to rationalize the disorder of *Almond,* in spite of (or because of) which its polemical bite and opportunistic energy remain undiminished. If radical dislocation and irresolution remain characteristic of Nashe's work (or of his personae), the cause is at least partly suggested by *Almond:* no single decorum, voice, or position can legitimately prevail. A version of negative capability thus manifests itself in his work, making it impossible for us to identify Nashe, or even for "Nashe" to identify himself, with any fixed or final position. The speaker of *Almond,* who appears under the comic name of Cuthbert Curryknaves, appears on both sides of the issue, that of hierarchical order and restrictive authority as well as that of carnivalesque folly and indecorum.

If I have introduced the term *negative capability* with some hesitation, it is because of the evident danger that it will be understood simply to idealize a divided or irresolute state of mind, and because it may too comfortably imply a fertile capacity to withold commitment in the face of balanced or equal alternatives. A liberal-utopian valuation of ambivalence may all too easily be reintroduced under the name of negative capability. I have, however, retained the term in preference to such a one as *embodying contradictions* —whether of a political or psychological order—because a certain capacity to defer resolution, to capitalize on an indeterminate situation, and to play out contradictions reveals itself in Nashe's performance. Abandoning the *propria persona* of *The Anatomy of Absurdity* and the *Menaphon* preface, Nashe acquires a new degree of flexibility or "irresponsibility" in the inconsistent persona of Cuthbert. If this degree of license was conferred by the particular circumstances of the Marprelate controversy, Nashe did not revert to the constraints of an idealized *propria persona* when the controversy ended; as both Travis Summersgill and G. R. Hibbard have shown, the role played by Nashe in this controversy expanded beyond the bounds of the occasion and determined Nashe's posture in his prolonged war of words with Gabriel Harvey. Having acquired a relatively autonomous power in the conflict with Marprelate, Nashe did not relinquish it once the conflict ended, and he finally became a serious nuisance to his erstwhile patrons, in whose hands their "instrument" turned.

Not only did the Marprelate controversy emancipate Nashe as a performer, but, as Summersgill in particular has shown, the occasion facilitated a marked advance in Nashe's technical skill and control. What Marprelate offered was a rhetorical model of calculated indecorum, neither naively formal nor innocent of all proprieties. Summersgill draws attention, for example, to the increased colloquial force, syntactic flexibility, and theatricality of Nashe's writing in the encounter with Marprelate, marking all this as an advance on the technical plane.[22] This advance in practice is accompanied, however, by a new degree of self-consciousness on

34

Nashe's part and by an intensified concern about the nature and status of the performer.

On one hand, the acquisition of a new power in and of performance, a new popularity, enables Nashe to conceive, as Hibbard has partly suggested,[23] of a performing caste, a competitive fraternity, the values and interests of which may become divorced from (even inimical to) the interests supposedly represented:

> Well, come on it what will, Martin and I will allow of no such doinges; wee can cracke halfe a score of blades in a backe-lane though a Constable come not to part vs. [P. 342]

This fraternal rivalry of brawlers represents at least a potential threat to the maintenance of "legitimate" public order, here embodied in the repressive figure of the constable rather than in a figure of spiritual authority. Not only does the speaker reveal a sense of complicity with his antagonist, but also a new sense of "championship" that depends less on the representation of legitimate interests than on professional accomplishment and a position in the public eye:

> Write or fight, which you will, our champion is for you at all weapons, whether you choose the worde or the sworde, neither comes amisse to him, he neuer took his domesticall dissention in hand to leaue it so soon. [P. 356]

Ostensibly, this breathless, paratactic sentence parodies the vulgar style of the Puritan challenge to legitimate authority, and refers to Marprelate rather than to his opponent, yet both the power of irony and any real distinction between Marprelate and his opponent tend to disappear in the welter of unrelated pronouns. The speaker remains unstably poised between mockery and approval, between detachment from and identification with the posture of the champion. If negative capability is once again manifest in this hesitation, so at least is a recognition of the alternative represented by Marprelate. In literal terms, the sentence constitutes a program of action; it also makes the prolongation of "domesticall dissension" (of the agonistic situation) a necessary condition of the performer's continued power.

So much on the one hand, where Nashe conceives of performance as a source of power and of romantic status. What lies on the other hand is a continuing consciousness of style as a matter of appearances. In contrast to Robert Greene, whose style Nashe conceives as a form of modest attire, the author of the Marprelate tracts presents himself to the world in a "rusty superfices." "Rusty" in this context can imply both soiled and malcontent; paradoxically an indecorous and nonconforming style proves more effective than a decorous and conforming one. Nevertheless, the appearance is deceptive, in that it belies an inner reality capable of being exposed.

The exposure of the Marprelate author—the man behind the mask, the person dressed in a "rusty superfices"—becomes the supreme *coup de théâtre* of *Almond*. At the time of the conflict, John Penry, a Puritan polemicist, was widely suspected to be the author of the pseudonymous tracts, yet the continuing mystery of the author's identity contributed to their appeal. In unmasking Penry, Nashe may have sought to dispel the mystery; in doing so he was also able to portray Penry in mode of brutally grotesque comedy:

> Neither was this monster of Cracouia vnmarkt from his bastardisme to mischiefe: but as he was begotten in adultery and conceiued in the heate of lust, so was he brought into the world on a tempestuous daie, & borne in that houre when all planets wer opposite. Predestination, that foresaw how crooked he should proue in his waies, enioyned incest to spawne him splay-footed. Eternitie, that knew how aukward he shoulde looke to all honesty, consulted with Conception to make him squint-eied, & the deuill, that discouered by the heauens disposition on his birth-day, how great a lim of his kingdom was comming into the world, prouided a rustie superficies wherin to wrap him as soone as euer he was separated from his mothers wombe. [P. 365]

The figure thus brought to light is of course not "the real Penry" but a conventionalized figure of Evil incarnate. His biography, as Summersgill has shown, is a parodic saint's life, while the terms in which his nativity is cast not only parody astrological prediction but also perhaps the Apostles' Creed. For Evil to come into existence in an ideal universe, the order of which it cannot ultimately change, it is necessary that a mysterious derangement or quasi-parodic misappropriation of ideal forms occur; Evil, as embodied in Penry, is accordingly both absurd and unnatural. A process of de-formation, the responsibility for which is attributed to imma- terial agencies ("Predestination that foresaw . . . Eternitie that knew"), enables Penry to take on his bastard existence and charac- ter, which must immediately be veiled under a "rusty superfices."

What Nashe exploits in the conflict with Marprelate is the pre- sumptive contradiction between inner and outer, between appear- ance and essence, in order to achieve his theatrical unmasking. This representation of Penry, however, is implicitly self-reflexive insofar as Nashe, too, masquerades in a "rusty superfices." The bastardism of the popular performer—his guilty interiority—is at once constituted and betrayed by his very performance. The ac- quistion of rhetorical power coincides with a loss of innocence in more senses than one, since it not only entails a new manipulative- ness, sophistication, and artifice, but also because it depends upon the promotion of division and disorder, thus becoming allied to Evil. Without any "saving" end (such an end as Nashe might claim in opposing Marprelate on behalf of legitimate authority), perfor- mance threatens to become irredeemably scandalous, at once a betrayal of what university wit ideally stands for and an inescapable form of complicity with the powers of darkness.

Although Nashe romantically embraces principles of agonistic conflict and self-assertion—principles fundamental, no doubt, to any philosophy of rhetoric whatever[24]—he does not do so without critical self-consciousness and without any "memory" of the ideal from which such principles represent a departure. Nashe's work as a whole at once embodies and problematizes such principles, at times rising to the level of explicit critique. Our reading of Nashe in the hindsight conferred by Jonsonian comedy might, for ex- ample, suggest that the licensing of "humour" is not the prelude to unlimited self-affirmation and free invention, but rather a capitulation to idiosyncratic arbitrariness and mechanical self- repetition. It may even be the prelude to an unrestrained obsessive- ness inimical to wit, making the performer ultimately the slave of his own rhetoric. Not only is compulsiveness evident on a massive and irredeemable scale in Nashe's work, but his own consciousness of this, together with his consciousness of the sadomasochistic

37

underside of romantic agon, enables him to project his own vision of the hell of "rhetoric."

In *Pierce Pennilesse*[25] the speaker vainly interrogates his fictional interlocutor, the Knight of the Post, concerning the true nature of that hell about which speculation is so rife:

> Would [you] acquaint mee with the state of your infernall regiment: and what that hel is, where your Lord holdes his throne; whether a world like this, which spirites like outlawes doo inhabit, who, being banisht from heauen, as they are from their Country, enuy that any shall bee more happy than they; and therefore seeke all meanes possible, that Wit or Arte may inuent, to make other men as wretched as themselues; or, whether it be a place of horror, stench and darknesse, where men see meat, but can get none, or are euer thirstie and readie to swelt for drinke, yet haue not the power to taste the coole streames that runne hard at their feet: where (*permutata vicissitudine*) one ghost torments another by turnes. [Pp. 217–18]

Both "wit" and "arte" exist here solely as invidious means to the general end of intensifying misery; hell becomes the place of depraved art and degenerate play (agon reduced to tormented compulsion). It must of course be said that this is the hell envisaged by Pierce Pennilesse, a *city* figure whose performance leaves him as "penniless" as before, and that "hell" implies the loss or inacessibility of a saving *pastoral* locality or form ("the coole streames that runne hard at their feete"). Pierce Pennilesse is also, however, an autobiographical role played by Nashe, and it may be taken, if not to represent the whole truth of his condition, then at least a certain understanding of his own predicament. Antipastoral and antiromance conceptions of rhetorical performance shape Nashe's career from the time of his preface to Greene's "Arcadian *Menaphon*," and the omnipresence of hell threatens to become the penalty for a sophisticated rejection of pastoral. Yet allowing even for this, the "demonic" rhetoric of Pierce Pennilesse lends itself to understanding in terms of a neoplatonic mythology in which rhetoric as such is a form of evil.

An initial banishment—from "heauen" and "their Country"—must be posited to account for the decay of vital "spirites" into melancholy "ghosts" in whom only the memory of a better order survives. The persistence of the spirit only in this diminished, negative guise becomes the assumed penalty of its departure from its "proper" and "original" location. Following this moment of alienation, which entails the loss of an ideal locality as well as of full spiritual being, a romantic outlaw role may be attempted—as may that of the railing satirist in *Pierce Pennilesse*—yet a consciousness of impotence, of cruel absurdity, and of tormented compulsion accompanies these performances. The hell envisaged by Pierce Pennilesse is either that of the miserable tormentor or that of the cruelly tormented, complementary places and complementary roles that constitute a total condition of the damned, and from which no exit is envisaged (*permutata vicissitudine*).

In the next chapter I shall revert to some of the issues implicit in this conception of hell. For the moment I intend only to establish that the power of performance with which Nashe is generally (also appreciatively and correctly) credited entails for him a consciousness of loss and of misapplied power. "Play," whether theatrical or rhetorical, does not necessarily imply any emancipation or freedom of self-fashioning, but may on the contrary imply enslavement to forms of necessity experienced as alien to the self. These motifs are never absent in Nashe's work, and they appear in even more drastic guises than they do in *Pierce*. *Christ's Tears over Jerusalem* supplies an instance.[26]

This work, itself an enormous monologue, is characterized by two inset orations, one spoken in the person of Christ and the other spoken in the person of Miriam, the woman who, during the siege of Jerusalem in A.D. 70, was forced by starvation to eat her own child. (This incident is often referred to in didactic literature of Nashe's period as a cautionary example of what may happen if the will of God is resisted for too long.)

Ostensibly, the fate of Jerusalem—a Roman siege followed by the destruction of the city—results from the citizens' failure to acknowledge the divinity and saving mercy of Christ. The fully exemplary victim, it would seem, is Miriam, whose quasi-Thyestean banquet represents the visitation, even upon the most seemingly innocent, of God's righteous anger. It also represents her fate in an unredeemed world, in which blind, literal necessity alone may prevail. Indeed, Miriam's feast becomes a cruel literalization of Christian communion (feeding on the body of the son) as well as a grotesque parody of Holy Family relations.

Nashe's treatment of this incident differs from that of his contemporaries in its sophisticated, self-advertising artistry. Instead of merely narrating the episode, he devises an elaborate speech for Miriam, who justifies her action at length before performing it and then again afterward when she is confronted by a greedy rabble who wish to share in the feast. Miriam's forensic performance becomes conspicuous in its resourcefulness and ingenuity, and it—rather than immediate necessity—facilitates the unthinkable action she performs.

Inherently, it might seem that the "case" of Miriam lends itself to a certain casuistry. Although implicated in the collective guilt of the city, she nevertheless commits the ultimate crime under pressure of dire need. Her culpability appears debatable. It is Miriam herself, however, who makes the case in her own favor, pleading her cause even before proceeding to the act. The following passage is characteristic:

> Euen as amongst the *Indians* there is a certaine people, that when any of their Kins-folkes are sicke, saue charges of physicke, and rather resolue (vnnaturally) to eate them vppe, then day-diuersifying Agues or blood-boyling surfets should fit-meale feede on them; so do I resolue, rather to eate thee vp, my sonne, and feed on thy flesh royallie, then inward emperishing Famine shoulde too vntimely inage thee.... Though *Dauid* sung of mercy and iudgement together, yet cannot I sing of cruelty and compassion together; remember, I am a Mother, and play the murdresse, both at once. [P. 72]

Miriam's speech is in more than one sense a rhetoric of purported innocence. As euphuistic parody, it represents the "innocent" rhetoric from which Nashe makes an early departure;[27] it also purports to establish Miriam's essential innocence in what is to follow.

The speech, however, is palpably sophisticated and is even set apart within the text by quotation marks, which isolate it for inspection. It becomes a tour de force of (special) pleading in which it is not the lack but the abundance of justifications that becomes suspicious. Not only does rhetoric mediate between her desire and her action, but she continuously shifts the grounds of her argument to encompass every possible point in her favor. (The Indians do it regularly . . . unnecessary expense will be saved . . . the child will not be prematurely aged by famine, but will die painlessly in the fullness of infancy . . . a royal banquet will ennoble the child. . . .) The act will either be one of pure altruism on the mother's part, or, should it after all remain an unnatural or guilty act, it will not be performed in the person of a mother, but rather in the alien person of a murderess.

Later on, Miriam will claim that she is obliged to play a variety of male roles alien to her essential being, including that of God the Father, who sacrificed his own son. Guilt will always attach itself to others. At one point Miriam addresses to the child the remark that "the enemies without and within shall divide thy bloods-guilt between them" (p. 74); the child itself is not necessarily excluded from this "division," since, should any trace of guilt remain, it may even inhere in the child itself ("thy bloods-guilt"). With more pathos than consistency, Miriam at another point assumes the role of the child's advocate, ostensibly pleading on its behalf and proclaiming its all-redeeming innocence. In short, Miriam protests a great deal too much. Both the nature of the arguments and their excess progressively incriminate her, or at least leave her trapped in the bind that opposes the rhetorical skill of pleading to the fact of innocence.

Miriam's is a forensic art of persuasion that legitimizes the unthinkable and betrays its own duplicity. Her facile word coinage, euphuistic balance, learned analogies, and tortuous conceits ("The foreskinne of original sin shalt thou clean circumcize by this one act of pietie" [p. 74]) are quite simply incompatible with her claim to essential innocence. The function of her rhetoric in facilitating the unthinkable soon becomes apparent, as does the abrupt defeat of "natural" maternal love; the words virtually speak themselves at the prompting of hunger:

> At one stroke (euen as these words were in speaking) she beheaded him, and when she had done, turning the Apron from of her own face on his, that the sight might not afreshly distemper her, without seeing, speaking, deliberating, or almost thinking any more of him, she sod, rost, and

41

powdred him; and hauing eaten as much as suffised, sette vp the rest.
[P. 75]

Following this banquet, it remains for Miriam to present herself on
stage. Confronted by the starving, "sedicious" rabble drawn by the
scent of food, Miriam puts into practice the strategy she has previously announced, that of dividing the "bloods-guilt" among her
enemies (who will otherwise rend *her* to pieces). Her own action,
along with the accompanying guilt, must be projected onto others:

> Eate, I pray you, heere is good meate, be not afrayd, it is flesh of my
> flesh.... Beholde his pale perboyld visage, how pretie-pitteous it
> lookes. His pure snow-moulded soft fleshe will melt of it selfe in your
> mouthes: who can abstaine from these two round teat-like cheeks?....
> Crauens, cowards, recreants, sitte you mute & amazed? Neuer entred
> you into consideration of your crueltie before? [Pp. 75–76]

This modest proposal successfully incriminates its destined victims, transferring the guilt of the self-interested performer to the
onlookers (or readers). In failing to recognize the performance for
what it is, the brutal but naive onlookers are simply taken in. Indeed, they are transfigured, losing their character as passionate
rebels and becoming frozen embodiments of rectitude:

> The Rebels hearing this, were wholy metamorpizd into mellanchollie;
> yea, the Chief-taines of them were overclowded in conceite. Was neuer
> till this euer heard from *Adam*, that a woman eate her owne Childe.
> [P. 77]

Exempting herself entirely, Miriam makes her hearers the subject
of her improvised—and plagiarized—morality play, binding them in
guilty communion. She invites all hearers to accept an allegedly
mnemonic taste of the child for whose death they now bear responsibility:

> Eate of my sonne one morsel yet, that it may memorize against you, ye
> are accessary to his dismembring. Let that morsell be his hart if you
> will, that the greater may be your conuictment. [P. 76]

The effect of Miriam's self-serving performance is to convict all
those present but herself of a monstrous crime—virtually an origi-

42

nal sin, unheard of "from Adam." Its effect is also to incriminate her, both in the eyes of the knowing reader and in reality, since it becomes the means by which evil nature triumphs over good.

The Jerusalem in which Miriam eats her own son might legitimately be designated a hell or perhaps an antiworld in which all too literally the flesh prevails. The allusions to Christian communion and to the redeeming role of the child clearly mark the loss or absence of the spritual dimension (the divine presence) in Miriam's Jerusalem, while the power of the word becomes allied to the satisfaction of bodily hunger. Miriam not only seduces herself into violating an ostensibly natural taboo, but opportunistically turns her weapons against her enemies, evoking the conscience that makes cowards of them all. In Jerusalem's war of all against all, Miriam (an unsanctified Mary) becomes the star performer and conspicuous survivor.

At this point it may seem absurd to revert to the question of Miriam's innocence, yet there is still a way in which that question is pertinent. Starvation is the given under which Miriam acts, and if her words enable her to eat (at whatever "human" cost) they may become the agents of a true necessity in the face of which guilt is beside the point. This possibility cannot be dismissed, and it is one that at least implies the pure luxury of higher feelings and of the spiritual sense as opposed to the literal. If necessity applies within the human sphere, it may do so in the most embarrassingly literal sense. Beyond this ineradicable possibility, however, which would yoke "rhetoric" to ultimate necessity, it remains to be considered whether Miriam is the victim or the manipulator of her own rhetoric. The reading I have attempted implies that conscious forensic cynicism (or at least knowingness) enters into Miriam's performance, which appears guilty to the informed onlooker. Yet it may also, by its superabundant pleading, reveal Miriam's conviction of her own guilt, thus making it "guilty" in a different sense. (We have no privileged access to Miriam's consciousness.) A "guilty" rhetoric may thus imply alternative possibilities, that of cold manipulativeness and that of relentless self-betrayal. The situation of the performer in relation to his or her own performance remains undecidable both here and elsewhere in *Christ's Tears,* drawing attention to a recurrent critical problem in the interpretation of rhetorical performance.

In this chapter I have examined some instances of "unredeemed rhetoric," attempting to suggest how such a rhetoric comes into being in Nashe's particular case and also to suggest how the redeeming of rhetoric (with all that that would imply) can become an imperative for Nashe and many of his peers. In the next chapter I shall try to develop this point, focusing particularly on the oration of Christ in *Christ's Tears* as the alternative to Miriam's oration. This alternative implies the possibility of a guilty rhetoric's redeeming or overcoming itself, becoming the speech of divine power rather than of human evil or limitation. All this is put at stake in Nashe's extraordinary impersonation of Christ.

CHAPTER 3

THE REDEMPTION
OF THE CITY

At the end of the previous chapter, I anticipated the moment in which Nashe would seek to redeem both rhetoric and the rhetorical persona from themselves. His doing so would, I suggested, entail no denial or repudiation of rhetoric, but rather their self-overcoming. This is the attempt that I shall examine in the present chapter. Before going on to consider the relevant works, however, I shall dispose of a few preliminaries.

An attempt to moralize his own rhetoric is evident in many of Nashe's works from *The Anatomy of Absurdity* (1588) onward. Guided partly by changes in literary taste and in the nature of the literary audience,[1] Nashe attempts (without sacrifice of rhetorical power) to play fashionable didactic and satirical roles. Hence Nashe's Elizabethan reputation as the "English Juvenal"; hence too his adoption of the jeremiad as a form and his playing the part of a railing preacher in such works as *Pierce Pennilesse* and *Christ's Tears*. In these antagonist roles, a rhetoric of power is at least theoretically compatible with disinterestedness and legality, while irrational violence becomes *saeva indignatio*. To adopt Nashe's own characteristic terms, the "retailing" of such works might be "profitable" in more senses than one, thus eliminating the contradiction between the mercenary and the ideal motive, between a self-affirming power and a self-sacrificing righteousness.

Needless to say, this conjunction remains to be desired. In *The Anatomy of Absurdity*,[2] in which the speaker adopts the persona of a learned anatomist in order to inveigh against the proliferating

45

absurdities of his world, Nashe is already haunted by the suspicion that "the ignorant goe by the direct way to heauen" (p. 49). The learned, humanistic speaker, at all events, while attempting to uphold the proprieties in an absurd world, becomes himself the ultimate figure of absurdity:

> And thus I ende my Anatomie, least I might seeme to haue been too tedious to the Reader in enlarging a Theame of Absurditie. [P. 49]

The speaker, in short, becomes a bore. Moreover, in opposing himself to absurdity, the speaker can only "enlarge" its "Theame," while as anatomist he becomes progressively infected with the disease. The phenomenon of the world's absurdity finally comes home to him. In doing so, it seemingly discredits the rhetoric of the learned jeremiad, a rhetoric implicated in absurdity, and even in grotesque absurdity if the fool should persist in his folly.

From the start, then, Nashe's rhetorical personae (whatever their verbal brilliance or power to entertain) are conscious of their own vitiating complicity in whatever they oppose. (Perhaps even of their ultimate responsibility for the states of affairs they denounce, whether these states involve absurdity or actual Evil as embodied in the figures of the Seven Deadly Sins.)[3] The vision of a hell of depraved art, included in the previous chapter, comes from the quasi-didactic *Pierce Pennilesse*,[4] and it is a hell that the speaker inhabits even before he knows it. Moreover, the didactic power of rhetoric is foreclosed, as the structure of *Pierce Pennilesse* implies. Although written against the devil and all his works, *Pierce* must in such a world as this address itself as a beggar's petition *to* the all-powerful devil. The devil accordingly becomes a kind of antipatron, to be cajoled and abusively flattered by a crazy speaker. Only those effects that are entertaining or subtly flattering are therefore permissible, while the redemptive or transforming energies of language are thwarted. Ostensibly didactic writing thus takes on a debilitating consciousness of its own theatricality, its own pandering to an audience, and its own impotent virtuosity. Precisely to the extent that a consciousness of its own "entertainment value" increases, so does its melancholy.[5] The work also becomes interminable in principle, bound as it is to the production of successive effects, not the achievement of a goal. *Pierce Penni-lesse* merely stops short when the speaker says: "And so I end this endlesse argument of speech abruptlie" (p. 245).

In what mode, then, can a self-overcoming be conceived? Given the presuppositions of Nashe and his contemporaries, the answer might be "only in a poetic mode." It is a commonplace in modern criticism that there is no definite line separating rhetoric from poetics in Renaissance literary theory; poetics cannot separate it-self from rhetoric, though it may sublimate rhetoric. While the *figures* remain common, the motives, the decorum, and the ends may become rarefied. Ideal motives (of the erected wit) supplant forensic motives (of the infected will); specifically poetic and generic criteria of decorum supplant those of mere oratory; and the ends of the work (as indicated in Sidney's *Apologie*) become those of didactic praise and blame rather than of mere disputation or play. In order to support the poetic undertaking, such entities as wit, imagination, and inspiration may be invoked, each of these terms being understood in its particular historical mode.

All this is familiar to readers of Renaissance literature, and I summarize in this fashion simply to review the preconditions of Nashe's undertaking. It may also pertinently be said that, on the basis of Sidney's *Apologie,* the poetic does not necessarily entail versification, but can manifest itself in verse and prose alike. The essential poetic qualities of "making" and edification do not depend on rhyme or meter. Furthermore, in the "golden" era of which Sidney's *Apologie* is the major theoretical expression, the aureation of language becomes in practice if not in theory a requisite of poetry.

In inventing a speech for Christ in *Christ's Tears,* Nashe relies upon aureation, but also on divine "inspiration," "*energia,*" a strict decorum of the divine "person," and on other devices that might be designated poetic.[6] The veiled, extreme, and extremely incongruous violence of this speech may thus be considered a good or sublimated violence. There is a place, in other words, for a poetic force that will finally prevail in the service of good ends. Yet if in various ways the speech of Christ announces itself as a prose poem, it appears that such a form, while uncontradictory for the Sidney of the *Apologie,* becomes a contradiction in terms for Nashe. He inflates various poetic devices to the point of absurdity[7]—even grotesqueness—while the speech remains a tour de force of rhetorical prose.

What underlies this phenomenon of poetic hypertrophy (and simultaneous breakdown) is the fact that for Nashe the poetic is at best a lost cause. It is not just that, for him, poetic pretensions are there to be seen through, but that it is in the nature of poetic brightness to "fall," and of poetic order to be experienced only in the moment of its loss. This loss of the poetic is enacted in Nashe's one surviving play, *Summer's Last Will and Testament* (1592), and it is enacted, although somewhat differently, in Nashe's one long surviving poem, "The Choice of Valentines" (otherwise known as "Nashe His Dildo"). Before moving on to *Christ's Tears,* I shall briefly consider the nature of this loss as manifested in "The Choice of Valentines." Once the full dimensions of the loss have been perceived, a just appreciation of *Christ's Tears* becomes possible.

What is lost in "The Choice of Valentines," along with an ideal poetic order, is an ideal pastoral order. These two orders (or ideas of order) are virtually coextensive for Nashe and his peers.[8] Although recoveries may be attempted, either under the guise of moral satire or in some paradoxical mode of urban pastoral, the prospects of full recovery remain questionable.

In "The Choice of Valentines," Nashe stages what he calls a "shift" to the city. In doing so, he continues to assign ontological priority to pastoral and to the poetic ideal, thus conferring by implication a diminished or "fallen" character upon the verse of the city. If this fall from grace also opens up new possibilities of literary urbanity, they are ones that Nashe cannot consistently realize, for reasons that appear in the course of the poem. The poem begins in a pastoral setting as a lover, speaking in the first person, sets out in quest of his "beloved saint." It turns out that the object of this romantic quest has already shifted to the city under somewhat compromising circumstances, and it is in the city that the lover traces her to a brothel. Before he can gain access to her, he is offered some inferior wares, and he discovers that a suitably high price has been placed on the services of a saint. (In Elizabethan parlance "saint" has the additional meaning "image of a saint.") The lover pays, and gains access to his mistress.

These preliminary transactions might seem to offer an occasion for the *saeva indignatio* of Juvenalian satire, yet the poem apparently seeks to locate itself in the urbane genre of the Ovidian elegy, in which a version of pastoral may resurface even in the tainted environment of a city brothel:

> A prettie rysing wombe without a weame,
>   That shone as bright as anie siluer streame;
> And bare out lyke the bending of an hill,
>   At whose decline a fountaine dwelleth still.
>   [3:408, 11. 109–12]

Pastoral survives, that is to say, in the erotic topography of the female body, and the shift to the city does not yet imply any radical loss or deformation. On the contrary, if we recall Donne's elegies, it may seem as though a threshold of inhibition has been crossed, and what lies beyond, at least for the male lover, is an America or new found land, which he may bestride like a colossus. In an almost direct inversion, the archaic role of the male lover as pilgrim and devotee may become that of the romantic conquistador, while the realm of the love poem may expand to encompass hitherto unknown material riches.

In Nashe's poem, however, the erotic world is not there to be possessed; if it exists, it has already been expropriated for commerce. Before he can approach his mistress he must bargain with the keeper of the establishment, and once past the threshold the speaker does not so much enter a new world as an erotic theater characterized by shifting and inscrutable appearances. In this theater his Mistress Frances performs and he will now perform. Left behind at the threshold is the world of pure essences and uncompromised beings.

The sexual act is then performed in successive styles or versions. After a certain initial stage fright, the male lover assumes the dominant role and enacts the heroic moment of male penetration in a pseudo-Chaucerian style of archaic potency:

> He rubd', and prickt, and pierst hir to the bones,
>   Digging as farre as eath he might for stones.

> Now high, now lowe, now stryking short and thick;
>   Now dyuing deepe he toucht her to the quick.

[11. 145–48]

As the act develops from its earthy beginnings, it becomes increasingly rarefied, and the process of copulation seemingly regenerates an entire cosmology of reciprocal love:

> He lyke a starre, that to reguild his beames
>   Sucks-in the influence of Phebus streames,
> Imbathe's the lynes of his descending light
>   In the bright fountaines of hir clearest sight.
> She faire as fairest Planet in the Skye
>   Her puritie to no man doeth denye.
> The verie chamber, that enclowds hir shine,
>   Looke's lyke the pallace of that God deuine,
> Who leade's the daie about the zodiake,
>   And euerie euen discends to th'Oceane lake.

[11. 159–68]

While copulation thrives, secure identities and differences are maintained within an ordered system. We pass in an ascending series, in which each term can safely stand for and imply the others, from *man* to *life* to *spirit* and to *God divine.* The original imbalance of an act initiated by the violence of male penetration remains traceable in the difference between "starre" and "planet," but that imbalance is progressively attenuated until the lovers meet in an ideal "midle waye" (1. 154).

While the power of copulation prevails, it sustains the true equivalence of the poem's insistent "likenesses" ("which lyke the sunne," "he lyke a starre") and also suspends equivocation about potentially ambiguous phrases, such as the one about the benevolent Venus who "her puritie to no man doth deny." The speaker, however, inhabits this illusory cosmos with self-conscious detachment, remaining a first-person spectator of his own third-person performance.

The act ends prematurely if predictably in this context with the speaker's inability to sustain physically his mythical male role. This failure wrings from him a question that is less purely rhetorical than it might be under other circumstances: "But what so firme that

50

may continue euer?'' The failure evokes from his mistress an elaborately stylized complaint about the inconstancy of the male and the instability of human joys. This complaint, too, has an unusually literal application in its context.

Succumbing as we no doubt will to the time-honored and consoling ritual of complaint, we will be unprepared for Mistress Frances's sudden revelation that she has anticipated the outcome. In fact, she possesses a dildo, which she proposes henceforth to substitute for mankind. This disclosure is withheld until three-quarters of the way through the poem and gains shock value from being sprung when we are likely to have been lulled by the platitudes of conventional melancholy.

The effect of the revelation is doubly and decisively to relegate the male lover to the position of an impotent voyeur, and at the same time to confront him with the power of artifice in an unsuspected, alien, and parodic form. The dildo, the appearance and mechanics of which are described in lavish detail, becomes a mocking image, not of what the male is, but of the lordly creature he would want to be. It is the unexpected confrontation with this artificial manikin and usurper that gives the speaker his cue for a satirical diatribe, but in a sense it is now (or always already) too late. What might have assumed the dignity of satire is reduced to an infantile tantrum, an outburst of pure jealousy, since the events of the poem have justified the dildo's existence. After this there is nothing left for the speaker to do except curse his own indiscretion in betraying a truly emasculating secret of women.

What are we to make of all this? Resorting to terms that may seem too grandiose in this context, we might say that the poem stages a radical dislocation and consequent loss of ontological security, not only for its speaker, but for love poetry as such. Mythical roles are now being played with a degree of self-consciousness that threatens to subvert them entirely, and a kind of anarchy or androgynous indifference threatens to overwhelm the poem at every stage. This danger is apparent not only in such disconcerting details as that of the woman's "mannely thigh," but in the constant ambiguity of pronoun referents, a feature of Nashe's work throughout his career. We might also recall that in this poem, unlike

Chaucer's Valentine's Day poem with which it invites comparison, there is no personified Nature to intervene in the end, underwriting for yet another year the guarantees for hierarchy, for "kind," and for symmetrical pairing. In the absence of that no doubt questionable personification, hierarchies collapse and oppositions are drastically short-circuited.

However, that is not all. Mythical roles are not so much played as played out in "The Choice of Valentines." The possibility of regenerating the play, or alternatively of recentering and reordering the love poem, comes to depend on an acknowledgment of the insatiability of female desire and on a recognition of the all-too-literal artifice that that desire calls into being. The Sidneyan fiction of the love poem, that there is an original surplus of male sexual desire and capacity necessitating a tireless art of persuasion, must be revised to take account of an original deficiency.

In the poem then, both love poetry and the status of artifice must be reconceived under a logic of primary insufficiency rather than one of primary excess. The consequences of this change are far-reaching; instructed by Derrida, we might safely assume that they are endless. I will not, therefore, try to pursue them to the end, but will draw some rapid conclusions before moving on.

First, the implication emerges from "The Choice of Valentines" that a logic of deficiency is *true* logic of the world, despite all claims to the contrary. The acknowledgment of that deficiency is so catastrophic in its consequences for any idea of benign order, whether natural or divine, that the betrayal of the secret is tantamount to the violation of a taboo. Better to keep up appearances, including the appearance of mourning for what merely cannot endure, than to acknowledge a primary deficiency resulting in an endless series of imbalances and compensatory artifices.

Second, female masturbation emerges not simply as a legitimate subject of love poetry but as its true and compelling subject—its secret subject, if you like. It is the limitlessness of female desire that turns the male partner into an anxious performer and then discloses an irredeemable deficiency of will; if the poem is to continue, it can only be about the autoerotic woman, and the male subject can remain in the poem only as a voyeur, making what he can of that embarrassing role.

Finally, the nature of artifice must be reconsidered. I have already suggested that artifice ceases to be thinkable as the sublimated expression or agent of male desire; instead, it reemerges in alien guise as the artifice of women, an artifice no doubt vulgar, materialized, even crudely mimetic, but still unassailably justified. Paradoxically, the low imitation supplants the deficient original, of which it becomes a mockingly substantial and superior image. Artifice thus moves from a secondary or marginal role into a primary one, from which it cannot legitimately be ejected. At this point we may say that the scandal is complete.

I recognize that these are sweeping conclusions and that I have spoken loosely about the love poem and love poetry. I might pass the buck by saying that "The Choice of Valentines" exemplifies Nashe's quixotic absolutism and straining at limits; it is as if the poem aspires to be an anatomy of love poetry in all its phases rather than a specimen of a particular kind. However, even a finely tuned account of the poem, which might emphasize the generic alternatives between which it hesitates, would still have to reckon with its particular character. The poem embodies a destablizing shock of recognition, and the effect of that shock is to give a peculiar uneasiness to the poem's wit. The poem's tonal, stylistic, and generic uncertainties are never resolved, nor is Nashe at any level the master of the situation. The effects of the impotence, anxiety, and resentment embodied *in* the poem are visible in the unrecuperable—or unrecuperated—disorder *of* the poem.

If "The Choice of Valentines" and its impotent persona cannot redeem themselves—unless pornographically—they nevertheless establish the shift to the city as a moment of profound dislocation and loss. The city emerges not as positive material or social entity to be written "about," but always paradoxically as a place of deficiency and negation:[9] deficiency of the divine poetic-creative will; deficiency of the word; deficiency of the natural order. The more prolific the city, the more the privation is felt. The mere existence of the city threatens to make this deficiency permanent, or to reveal it as permanent. Such deficiency will then no longer be the temporary (if prolonged) outcome of a "fall" that will fortunately be rectified, but will rather reveal itself as the primary, determining, and irrevocable condition of the world. In reality, there will have been no fall, but only a contingent, shifting, and artificial state of existence in time. What precedes the so-called fall is not an Edenic condition of the world, but rather a state of ignorance or self-deception from which an awakening is possible. In reality the city, however temporal, material, disorderly, and unjust, threatens to reveal its eternal character, preempting and disqualifying pastoral-poetic origins.

Such are the prospects that open up with "The Choice of Valentines." Psychologically they may be intolerable prospects, regenerating as a "reaction formation" the grand ideas of pastoral and of poetic order. Shakespearean romance is perhaps best understood in this mode of reaction-formation.[10] For Nashe, the "recovery" remains an even more problematical gamble than it is for Shakespeare, partly because the erosion of the poetic in his work is so catastrophic.

The recovery depends at one level on the transformation of victim into hero. What Nashe's rhetorical personae almost always embody is a consciousness of loss and victimization: the anatomist of the absurd becomes its spokesman; the university wit becomes the devil's victim; the persona of "The Choice of Valentines" becomes the victimized lover. Nashe's consciousness of the martyred role is evident in *The Unfortunate Traveller* (the title is enough), in which he identifies himself in a humorous moment with St. Thomas of India. In *Lenten Stuff*, he appears literally as a fugitive from the law.[11] In *Christ's Tears*, Nashe identifies himself with the ultimate victim, but one in whom a divine power of recovery is also embodied. The Christ of *Christ's Tears* undertakes both to save the city and to save himself.

Before considering this relatively unfamiliar work, I shall briefly recapitulate its structure and content. In *Christ's Tears*, Nashe adopts a didactic persona akin to the one he adopts in *Pierce Pennilesse*, that of a railing preacher denouncing the vices and corruptions of the city. In one phase of *Christ's Tears*, however, the preacher puts off his own person and assumes that of Christ, at the same time adopting and carrying to unparalleled extremes of violence and elegant variation the rhetoric of the jeremiad. The work as a whole comprises three distinct sections.

In the first one, after invoking divine inspiration, the preacher sets the scene for his own oration spoken in the person of Christ. He emphasizes both the power and mercy of Christ, and then, putting off his own person, assumes that of Christ. In that person, he delivers an inordinate, threatening appeal to the citizens of Jerusalem to mend their ways before it is too late. The preacher then reassumes his own person.

In the second, the preacher describes the consequences of Jerusalem's failure to heed Christ's plea. Forty years after the death of Christ, the Jews rebel against their Roman overlords, and the city simultaneously experiences an internal political disruption. As a result both of internal anarchy and of a siege by the Roman armies, starvation sets in. The exemplary victim of the city is Miriam. In fact, starvation becomes the exemplary punishment inflicted on the city for its failure to heed Christ's appeal. Finally, as Christ foreknew, the evil city is annihilated and the temple destroyed.

In the final section, the preacher warns the citizens of London not to tempt providence as the Jews did, reverts to the topic of the Seven Deadly Sins, and concludes with a prayer for mercy.

My main concern is the first section, particularly the address spoken in the name and person of Christ. This section cannot, however, be read in complete isolation. In the second or "historical" section, Nashe draws freely on one or more popular English versions of Joseph Ben Gorion's ninth- or tenth-century account of the destruction, in A.D. 70, of Jerusalem and its temple by the imperial armies of Titus. In using this account as he does, Nashe situates himself in a naively didactic "literature of warning," in which the fall of one great city prefigures that of another unless it will mend its ways.[12] The point of this didactic literature is to avert judgment, or to prevent history from repeating itself. The fall of Jerusalem appears frequently in didactic literature of the period as a vindication of divine justice and as a prefiguration of the fate London is bringing upon itself.

What sets Nashe's work apart from works in the same didactic genre is its manifest sophistication—a term that, in this context, ceases to be complacently honorific, reverting rather to its moral dubiousness and to its intimate connection with rhetorical debasement in the Elizabethan lexicon. The effect of Nashe's "sophistication" of the naive form is to make it both self-advertising and self-questioning. His linking Ben Gorion's text to the Bible, as well as his "reading" the fall of Jerusalem in the light of prophecy and revelation, renders both the identity of Christ and operations of divine providence highly problematical. If it is possible to read Jerusalem's fate in the light of biblical prophecy, it now becomes equally possible to read biblical prophecy in the darkness of its historical fulfillment; a newly sophisticated intertextuality prevails. In particular, the biblical figure of Christ, who sheds his unavailing tears over an unrepentant and irredeemable Jerusalem, becomes baffling and contradictory, even susceptible to drastic reinterpretation. The consequences of Nashe's sophistication become fully apparent during the oration of Christ, but the newly problematical relationship between Christ and the city, or more broadly between the divine and the historical, begins to generate conflicting scenarios within the work.

The fate of Jerusalem may, for example, come to imply Christ's inability to redeem the city, the destruction of which he then resentfully wills despite a hypocritical and disarming flow of tears. It may also suggest that Christ brings no new dispensation, but is a jealous god in a newly deceptive—even effeminate—guise, in which case the New Testament becomes a thinly disguised version of the Old Testament, which is that of a jealous god. The latter possibility surfaces when Nashe-as-preacher cites the Old Testament text: "The Lord is known in executing judgment" (Psalm 9). Here *known* comes under pressure, since it may confirm the suspicion that divine compassion is a misleading appearance; it also makes a definitive act of execution the sole reliable manifestation of divine identity. The omnipotent Christ, who effectively wills the destruction of Jerusalem, thus begins to be invested with the human psychology of an Othello, that demigod moving mildly and lovingly among men, but jealously reasserting himself and making himself known (even if not quite as he would want to) in executing judgment. "This sorrow's heavenly; it strikes where it doth love."

If, however, Christ is *not* the true son of a jealous God, perhaps he is humanly impotent, which would explain his failure to redeem his chosen city and people, not to mention his failure to save himself. The forty years that elapse between Christ's death and the destruction of the city are enough to weaken the causal linkage. (*Post hoc non ergo propter hoc.*) Given this lack of temporal and causal immediacy, the fate of Jerusalem as an instance of divine retribution must be reasserted through the distorting and even opaque medium of signs and portents:

> GOD thought it not enough to haue threatend them by his Sonne, but he emblazond the ayre with the tokens of his terror. No Starre that appeared but seemd to sparkle fire. . . . Ouer the Temple . . . was seene a Commet most coruscant . . . which in his mouth (as a man in his hand) all at once he made semblance as if hee shaked and vambrasht. . . . Whole flockes of Rauens (with a fearefull croking cry) beate, fluttred, and clasht against the windowes. A hideous dismal Owle . . . in the Temple-porche built her nest. [Pp. 60–61]

The providence (let alone the justice) of a now absent deity can reassert itself only in this bizarre rhetoric of signs and semblances, the ludicrous excess and melodramatic banality of which defy serious interpretation. These are either the lavish effects of a pagan theater, signifying nothing and lending themselves both to cynical parody and to exploitation, or else they darkly signify the presence of a mad revenger about to reveal himself in the *coup de théâtre* of the final act. If God is involved at all, he can be so only in the double guise of the vindictive father (Hieronymo) and the innocent, murdered son.

And that is not the only conceivable meaning of the historical melodrama of Jerusalem. If there is after all no God to whose power the fate of Jerusalem testifies, the place of such a God remains to be filled, as it duly is by the power of the imperial city. If the fate of Jerusalem does *not* reveal the power of a jealous God chastizing his chosen people, it reflects the omnipotence of Rome, of Caesar rather than God. Having attempted to cast off the mild yoke of Roman despotism, Jerusalem is besieged, its temple is destroyed, and its people are dispersed. All this may have proto-typical implications for a hubristic English Protestant common-wealth (a "temple-boasting people"), which, like that of the Jews, believes itself to be the object of a special providence. In any case, the play of providential history gives way to the drama of Roman power.

It is not my aim to trace out the various scenarios embodied in *Christ's Tears,* but rather to suggest how deeply problematical and even contradictory Nashe's sophistication renders his didactic material. The possibility of a coherent or fully consistent representation of the baffling figure of Christ recedes, yet Nashe perseveres in the attempt against all odds. What remains at stake is still the possibility of redeeming the city, of reasserting a "divine" power of eloquence, and of reconstituting literary identity, not as that of the impotent performer, but as that of the one truly saving presence within the city.

It would appear, then, that in *Christ's Tears* Nashe attempts, even if not *in propria persona,* to assume a major role in his own time and on the big stage of the world. His doing so gives rise to the superficially contradictory fact that the presence of Christ is staged in the most uncompromisingly contemporary terms; Nashe brings to the impersonation of Christ the highest powers and ethical pretentions of Tudor humanist rhetoric in "poetic" guise—its figures, its devices, its alleged capacity for exemplary imitation, and its alleged force of moral persuasion. The speech of Christ becomes a bizarre showpiece of precocious virtuosity.

To quote Nashe's own academic terminology, he "supposes" Christ in a "continued oration" addressing the citizens, and these terms alone mark the oration as a tour de force of university wit. Although the speech is based on certain biblical utterances of Christ—utterances that are continuously woven back into the oration—the whole fantastic diatribe is a gigantic amplification of what Christ is recorded to have said, and is thus again marked as a virtuoso display. Nashe also uncharacteristically tries to mark the boundaries of speech and persona, thus upholding a technical decorum. In short, the speech of Christ comes closer than anything

Nashe ever wrote to identifying *itself* as pure rhetoric, and to asserting the pure force of rhetoric.

The convertibility of that pure rhetoric into an authentic manifestation of the divine will depends for Nashe primarily on the power of poetic invocation, and secondarily on Augustinian precedent; in *Christ's Tears* Nashe extensively cites the Augustine of the *Confessions* and repeats the Augustinian maxim "The Word of God, be it preacht by Hipocrite or Saint, is the Worde of God, and not be dispised or disanuld" (p. 20). For Nashe the propagation of the Word in the person of Christ thus becomes a form of licensed folly.

I would suggest that Nashe's playing the moralist in *Pierce Pennilesse* becomes overtly a version of playing the fool; here I would argue that his playing Christ becomes a manifest instance of *folie de grandeur*. Nashe presents on a large scale the disturbing spectacle of the fool rushing in. If the outcome appears to be a triumph of grotesque vulgarization and naive hubris, the attempt may nevertheless call the common bluff. What makes this *serious* folly intolerable is its power to expose the shoddy diplomacy, the compromising decorum, and the impure artfulness that characterize more acceptable enterprises. In other words, the presence of such folly is seriously embarrassing, constituting a challenge to any temporizing decorum or to any "lesser" form of seriousness.

The challenge this performance presents is, moreover, double; its apparent naïveté may reappear on consideration as an extreme form of cynicism. It is difficult to avoid the suspicion that *Christ's Tears* is a gigantic hoax sprung, not without malicious pleasure, on the God-fearing citizens of London, habitual consumers of tracts in the same genre. Nashe might seem to give the game away by alluding as he does to the text: "There shall arise false Christs, and false prophets, and they shall show great signs and wonders; insomuch, if it were possible, they shall deceive the very elect" (Matt. 24:23). In presenting his "profitable" discourse, Nashe seems to be inventing the role of the Jonsonian mountebank, so self-assured that he can warn those he is about to deceive of the presence of imposters. The preacher becomes not so much the good shepherd as the wolf in sheep's clothing.

The critical issue here is not so much that of choosing between a naive and a sophisticated interpretation of the same text, but rather of confronting the very existence of these alternatives. The effect of Nashe's extremism is to reduce "pure" rhetoric to the either/or of naive hubris and cynical fraud, the work of the fool or the work of the knave. Naively "poetic" high seriousness becomes inseparable, even indistinguishable, from cynical fraud, and these extremes encroach upon the middle, leaving no secure ground for an authentically serious art to occupy.

The literary-rhetorical predicament Nashe stages is at the same time a larger cultural predicament, the nature of which can be formulated in terms supplied by Huizinga's *Homo Ludens*. In that work Huizinga lumps together the inspired prophets, poets, shamans, and sorcerers of primitive society, claiming that it is their fate, as well as that of their ostensibly homogeneous communities, to be at once deceived and undeceived by sacred performances. It is that "saving" duplicity that constitutes and sustains the primitive community.

I am not concerned here with the anthropological validity of Huizinga's claim, or with his limiting it to primitive societies. I am concerned with his formulation of the principle that, while the quasi-priestly, quasi-poetic invocation and embodiment of the divine cannot fail to arouse suspicion of fraud, that process of invocation and embodiment remains the sole mode of access to divine power, and thus to the magical, restorative energies upon which the community relies. Civilized compromises and decorous substitutes will not necessarily suffice. The geometrical representation of divine order, for example, will not only imply the eternal absence of the divine, but will succumb to its own powerless abstraction. Similarly, the ritual celebration of the real presence may succumb to its own empty repetitiveness and theatricality. The Text as a revelation of the divine need only be seriously read to become, in Nashe's words, "a Minotaur's laborinth of pain euerlasting" (p. 79).

In attempting to dramatize and even embody the divine presence and will *in* history, particularly given the perceived impotence of ordinary preaching to the city, Nashe must proceed at the risk of stigmatizing himself as a foolish or cunning virtuoso; the very marks of "pure rhetoric" will become incapacitating stigmata. His attempt to embody the absolute, not merely in language, but in the rhetoric of his place and time, must therefore come to seem like a self-defeating compulsion. In *Christ's Tears,* however, the compulsion is played out to the bitter end.

To cut a long story short, the irresistible force of eloquence finally confronts the immovable object of the unredeemed city. Christ's rhetoric is reduced (or inflated) to a pure magic of incantation, a pure violence of repetition. Basing himself on a text from Matthew, the speaker declaims:

> O *Ierusalem, Ierusalem, that stonest,* and astoniest thy Prophets with thy peruersnesse, that lendest stonie eares to thy Teachers, and with thyne yron breast drawest vnto thee nothing but the Adamant of GODS anger: what shall I doe to mollifie thee? The rayne mollifieth harde stones: ô that the stormie tempest of my Teares might soften thy stony hart! Were it not harder then stone, sure ere this I had broken and brused it, with the often beating of my exhortations vpon it. . . . By the old Law, he that had blasphemed, r̄euiled his Parents, or committed adulterie, was *stoned* to death . . . thine Elders and Prophets thou *stonest* to death. . . . For this shalt thou grinde the *stones* in the Myll with *Sampson,* and whet thy teeth vpon the *stones* for hunger; and if thou askest anie man Bread, he shall gyue thee *stones* to eate. (Pp. 23–25)

Here, finally, the city as material entity and the city as human community coalesce in a single image of pure stone, against which the pure force of rhetoric seemingly beats in vain. The very resistance of the stone continuously reignites the rage of the word, while the violence of the word invites a further barrage of stones. The impasse appears complete. Moreover, the original deficiency of will to which I referred is now being overcompensated by an insane excess of will, which can only betray itself and thus revert to being a sign of impotence.

Not only does rhetoric fail in grandly exemplary fashion, but the mere prolongation of the attempt beyond all bounds of reason is not without consequences; Christ becomes the ultimate victim of his own self-incriminating rhetoric. He protests far too much, thus betraying his own sense of impotence, his own guilt, and his own violent resentment. Moreover, in amplifying Christ's biblical words, Nashe begins to arouse suspicions where they may never previously have existed. Although the preacher elaborately distinguishes between speech in his own impotent human "person" and speech in the divine "person" of Christ, the distinctions are progressively eroded.[13] The inadmissible lesson that begins to emerge from Scripture is that an all too human Christ could *not* redeem his chosen city and people, disciples notwithstanding.

On the face of it, the reason for Christ's failure was simply a tactical error. The deceptive mildness and humanity of his approach made it impossible for the people of the city to conceive of him as a figure of divine power. Neither the Jews nor their Roman overlords could take Christ seriously without a greater show of force. It becomes possible for Nashe (or his preaching persona) to correct this error, supplying Christ's rhetoric not with the substance but with the power it lacked. Before assuming the person of Christ, the preacher identifies him with Tamburlaine, whose siege of the city will always culminate in its utter annihilation if offers of mercy are rejected. The preacher tells us that certain biblical texts, properly construed, are like the red and black flags displayed to the unyielding cities Tamburlaine finally conquered. Having thus created the appropriate scenario for Christ's speech— and having compensated for Christ's misleadingly "pleasant approach"[14]—the performance may begin. This performance's legitimacy depends upon its being both potentially effective and on its being a correct "understanding" of what, on the basis of biblical and historical evidence, Christ might be "supposed" to have said. If what follows is ineffective or a misrepresentation, it can only draw attention to a continuing historical absence of the all-powerful Word that might save the city, averting its fate of violent extinction. A merely divine performance will not suffice, although it may betray the historical and psychological finitude of the performer.

The Christ of *Christ's Tears* emerges, not unpredictably, as the type of the "rhetorical" Renaissance superman. His performance, which is always derived by implication from the Gospel of Matthew, becomes that of a jealous God or of a paranoid madman who thinks he is God. He cannot be cleared of suspicion, nor can he clear himself; his attempted self-justifications merely compromise him more. He says, for example:

> I haue hearde quietly all thy vpbraydings, reproofes and derisions: as when thou saydst I was a drunkard, and possessed with a diuel, that I cast out diuels by the power of *Beelzebub*, the Prince of the diuels; that I blasphemed, was mad, & knew not what I spake: Nor was I any more offended with these contumelies, then when thou calledst me the son of a Carpenter. [P. 23]

Here Christ's consciousness of the charges to which his actions give rise is not enough to dispose of the charges, since he will persist in his extravagant claims, continue staging miracles to justify them, and demand unlimited submission to his interminable "reproofes and upbraidings." Not only is Christ unable to convince his city audience of the validity of his claims, but he begins to reveal ever more clearly the psychology of his compulsion.

In denying that he is the son of a carpenter, Christ makes himself the son of a mythical but absent father whose part he wilfully attempts to play. In doing so he will not only attempt the show of force necessary to bring the city to its knees, but will come to identify that city with a cruel, denying mother whom he alternately woos and threatens, at the same time suspecting the presence of a more successful rival:

> *Ierusalem,* the Daughter of my people, I am sore vexed and compassionate for thee, *Ierusalem,* the midst of the earth, the mother of vs all, in the midst of whom I haue wrought my saluation. . . . O let me pitty thee, for I loue thee impatiently. . . . Sathan, refrayne thine odious embraces, the bosome of *Ierusalem* is mine: touch not the body contracted to me. [Pp. 21–22]

This psychopathology of the "impotent" son needs no analysis; it exposes itself, and I shall therefore not prolong the demonstration. What emerges from Nashe's representation of Christ is not only the fact that, but the reasons why, Christ cannot save the city, or save himself. The unredeemed way of the world, the language of the world, and the wisdom of the world prevail. In this world of the city, or, as Nashe's Puritan contemporary Thomas Beard would insist on having it, this theater of God's judgments, the Redeemer is an overambitious boy trying to do a man's work, while the Father remains a paranoid projection of the Son. In the city, the pastoral figure of Christ is without redeeming virtue; in the city likewise, it is the fate of the Messiah to be crucified.

CHAPTER 4

THE LYING PAGE

The issue of *Christ's Tears*—and it is one that implicates writers other than Nashe within the period—is not that of Marlovian atheism, but rather of the absolute alienation of the Word in and by rhetoric. Where rhetoric prevails, the Word is absent.[1] I have suggested that Nashe can only stage (play out) in *Christ's Tears* a felt deficiency that finally cannot be overcome, but the acceptance of which is attended by painful consequences. Nevertheless, certain adjustments to a world (and a language) without redemption prove possible. In the preface to the second edition of *Christ's Tears*, Nashe unmasks himself and at the same time recharacterizes the performance he has undertaken. The presence, unacknowledged throughout *Christ's Tears* but now triumphantly revealed, is that of the virtuoso. The relevant form of virtuosity is that of word coinage and compounding.[2] No longer identifying himself with the grand enterprise of salvation, Nashe now situates himself within a frankly mercenary economy, in which words become material rather than spiritual currency. Within this economy a new conception of the word becomes possible.

Most readers will notice the relentless production in *Christ's Tears* of what Nashe calls his "Italionate coyned verbes all in Ize" (p. 184): mummianize, anagrammatize, tyrannize, cabalize, Diagorize, oraculize, etc. It is possible also for the reader to have noticed the industrious compounding practiced in *Christ's Tears*: sinne-surfetted, long-breathed, full-butt, thought-exceeding, scare-bugge, clowde-climbing, Nazarite-tresses, sinne-gluttonie, eare-agonizing, heauen-gazing, woe-enwrapped, Temple-boasting, Outlaw-army, yeares-dimnesse, life-expedient, ayrie-bodied, water-mingled, sloth-

65

favoring, etc., etc. Nashe is also credited with a substantial number of coinages in *Christ's Tears:*[3] abhorrent, adumbrate, ambiguity, articulate, balderdash, circumduct, concise, congestion, controvert, devastation, dimunitive, expiate, multifarious, niggling, progeniture, vociferate, etc. Even if a reader has noticed all these peculiarities (which certainly advertise themselves), they will not necessarily "mean" anything until Nashe identifies them with a new persona and situates them in a new rhetorical "economy." This is what Nashe does in the preface to the second edition, at the same time implicity disavowing any other significance of *Christ's Tears.* A new model for transcendent performance is invoked:

> For the compounding of my wordes, therein I imitate rich man who, hauing gathered store of white single money together, conuert a number of those small little scutes into great peeces of gold, such as double Pistols and Portugues. Our English tongue of all languages most swarmeth with the single money of monasillables, which are the onely scandall of it. Bookes written in them and no other seeme like Shop-keepers boxes, that containe nothing else saue half-pence, three-farthings, and two-pences. Therefore what did me I, but hauing a huge heape of those worthlesse shreds of small English in my *Pia maters* purse, to make the royaller shew with them to mens eyes, had them to the compounders immediately, and exchanged them foure into one, and others into more, according to the Greek, French, Spanish and Italian? [P. 184]

In the beginning there is no longer the all-powerful (mythical) Word, but only a multitude of little native words; in this vacuum of the Word, the primitive material nature and material poverty of (the) language stand revealed. Not only is language kept in its original state of debasement by petty hoarding (shopkeepers' boxes)[4] and by functioning as the currency of a plebeian commonwealth, but its potential power remains unrealized for want of a manipulative genius. It is the original state of affairs, not a "fallen" one, that now constitutes the "scandall." Uninhibited by the guilt of departure from a mythically exalted origin, the performer is now free to (mis)appropriate the common currency, to convert it into the "gold" of international circulation, and to make it an object of appreciation "in mens eyes." In short, the aestheticization of language may now proceed unchecked by scruples, as may the self-aggrandizing activities of the performer. Moreover, it is speech's alienation from common forms and functions that reconstitutes it as an object of beauty.

Under this new aesthetic regime, it is no longer objectionable that the "show" exists merely to dazzle "mens eyes," nor is it objectionable that a royal show proceeds in the entire absence of royal substance. (Or if there is a "royal substance," it can now safely be identified with gold itself.) The golden world of Sidney's *Apologie* shifts to become that of *Volpone* and *The Alchemist*. A radical transvaluation of values is evident in Nashe's preface, in the course of which the enabling act is written for a noble disutility of language and for a show that simply is what it seems, there being nothing to hide. Scandal is not only embraced but boldly reversed.

Both intelligence and bravado, I would suggest, are required of Nashe if the prolonged fiasco of *Christ's Tears* is to be retrieved after the fact. For the work to reassume its character as a prose poem, it must be resituated in a paradoxical and "fallen" poetics, which no longer apologizes for itself. Poetic "making" as an image of divine creativity yields to poetic coinage and compounding in imitation of the "rich man" of the world.

The emancipation of the poetic from excessive respect for ideal *origins* proceeds in Nashe's new metaphors from gardening and pharmacology:

> You will, like the Apothecaries, vse more compounds then simples, and graft wordes as men do their trees to make them more fruitfull. [P. 184]

A positive and beneficial "sophistication" can be conceived once the tyranny of the ideal has been overthrown, and once "simples" are denied any magical efficacy. A truly sophisticated poetic will, in short, come to terms with its own fertile artifice, its own complex nature, and its own forms of power.

Such at least is the formula that seems to emerge in the preface to the second edition. By the time Nashe wrote this preface, however, he had already published *The Unfortunate Traveller*,[5] a work wholly different in character from *Christ's Tears*. It is as if the new poetics of Nashe's preface are superseded before they can take effect in his work, or as if they represent a blind alley for him. The tour de force of coinage and compounding remains the hallmark of *Christ's Tears,* a work virtually *sui generis,* and it is not in "Royallizing [his] Muses" (p. 60) that Nashe forges a career. The motifs of bravado and sophisticated reversal are, however, pertinent to *The Unfortunate Traveller.*

It is possible to call *The Unfortunate Traveller* "a matter of style" without grossly misrepresenting it. The work appears, at all events, to point nowhere beyond style, while in it Nashe achieves a quality of sheer performance that readers have always recognized. The technical basis of this preformance largely entails rhetorical amplification and figures of disorder (*hyperbaton*), while it excludes, for example, the mechanical process of word formation that appears in *Christ's Tears.* John Berryman's appreciation will adequately suggest the aesthetic appeal—as opposed to the purely technical character—of Nashe's "prose as prose." What also contributes to our sense that *The Unfortunate Traveller* is "a matter of style" is its parodic brilliance. Consciousness of style, together with its elevation of parodic excess, virtually typifies the work.[6] The inevitable comparisons with Sterne, Joyce, and Nabokov suggest themselves, while Nashe tempts us with the idea of a perennial modernism.

If style is the substance of *The Unfortunate Traveller,* it is so not simply on account of the self-advertising performance, but on account of Nashe's having consciously "liberated" style. Style no longer means either a demure conformity or a tormented Pride that compulsively "ad-dresses" itself without wanting to admit its true character. Carried to an unprecedented degree of extravagance, style paradoxically no longer covers up anything significant, and its self-parodying excess becomes compatible with a sophisticated bravado:

> For your instruction and godly consolation, bee informed, that at that time I was no common squire, no vndertrodden torch-bearer; I had my feather in my cap as big as a flag in the fore-top; my French dublet gelte in the bellie as though (like a pig readie to be spitted) all my guts had bin pluckt out; a paire of side paned hose that hung downe like two scales filled with Holland cheeses; my longe stock that sate close to my docke, and smoothered not a scab or leacherous hairie sinew on the calfe

68

of my legge; my rapier pendant like a round sticke fastned in the tacklings for skippers [bugs] the better to climbe by; my cape cloake of blacke cloth, ouerspreading my backe like a thorne-backe, or an Elephantes eare. [P. 227]

Jack Wilton, the child of the city, becomes in this passage a figure of brilliant decadence, insolently presenting himself "for your instruction and godly consolation." The inventory of his apparel no longer allegorizes Deadly Sin, as comparable inventories do in *Pierce Pennilesse,* but rather proclaims the man. More accurately, clothing enables the man to proclaim himself, its artful disarray covering "not a scab or lecherous hairie sinew." The contradiction or wholly negative relation between "style" and "content" is overcome, allowing the speaker to affirm himself boldly through the pronoun "I." Forsaking naked innocence, the speaker paradoxically recovers it to a degree by being what he seems and hiding nothing, not even the artfulness of his self-exposure. The heavy eroticization of style, moreover, enables it to "go beyond" mere puerile narcissism. A paradoxical recovery of style in a mode of fantastic excess therefore emancipates the Nashe of *The Unfortunate Traveller* to pursue "effects" without allegorical or didactic necessity. Admittedly, Jack Wilton is not Nashe *in propria persona,* yet he is a figure in whom Nashe can project a certain rhetorical self-consciousness.

I would suggest, however, that a stylistic model is a necessary but not sufficient condition for the understanding of *The Unfortunate Traveller.* Although the work is a matter of style, it is also an antiromance, first-person fictional narrative, and even a "critical fiction" of its period. On all these counts, the work calls for—and has received—recognition.[7] It also calls, as many readers have noticed, for a recognition of the page in its own right.

Forcing the issue a little, one might call *The Unfortunate Traveller* an informal phenomenology of the page: of its prehistory, its historical interlude, and its end. To put the issue in this way, however, is to speak a language alien to Nashe's period and to his own idiom. Proceeding more conservatively, let us recall that Nashe is credited in the *O.E.D.* as the first user of "page" in its sense of a printed sheet (in the *Menaphon* preface). Nashe's own usage thus enables him to confer a double identity on his page-protagonist Jack Wilton. The pun on page is not relentlessly pressed, but is always available, and it contributes to the work's self-conscious doubling back. The page is both a figure in the social hierarchy and a sophisticated liar whose "creditors" (p. 209) are always bound to be taken in. This page is never innocent, as its own self-conscious punning on pages as "privy tokens" (p. 208) implies. Instead of idealizing the page, Nashe remains mindful of its "fundamental" nature.

In his new preoccupation with the page, Nashe registers in its historical contingency *and* its antiidealistic implications the "migration" of rhetoric from its elevated situation in the court, the academy, and the pulpit to its new (low) situation in the city and on the printed page. To say this is to claim little more than has traditionally been claimed about Nashe's work, namely that its "whole point" lies in its exploitation of, and bondage to, the emergent technology of printing. What has also been recognized is that the loss of rhetorical altitude and good form is accompanied, in the case of Nashe and his peers, by a gain in humor, flexibility, and popular appeal. This is not all that is at issue, however. The self-conscious emergence of the page in its own right implies a radical, perhaps irrevocable, alienation of language from its supposedly primordial character as speech (from its ideal character); a "purely technical" phenomenon threatens to make an essential difference. It is Nashe's peculiar role, for which he is uniquely equipped in his period, to stage this debacle. The moment in which the page is foregrounded is one in which it ceases to be the invisible servant of a higher order of language and meaning, and assumes its own existence in a world in which it is no longer to be denied. Moreover, the endless succession of pages, constituting their own spurious order, threatens an infinite deferral of true order or ultimate significance.

In terms of my own argument, the self-conscious existence of the page exacerbates in the highest degree the ostensibly malign rhetoricity of rhetoric, supplying it with an enormously expanded "base," heightening its alienation, and licensing an entirely new range of effects (including typographical effects of the kind usually associated with Sterne, but which Nashe also trifles with in *Have with You to Saffron Walden*). The redeeming of the page becomes a problem of a different order from that of redeeming rhetoric in its pretechnological (though never untechnical) phase.

In *The Unfortunate Traveller*, the powers and privileges of the page are presented at first as parodic. The page is not fully self-generating, but acquires its own life when it emancipates itself from the pure duty of representation. It affirms itself, in other words, when it discovers in a moment of sophistication that it possesses a capacity for diverting mimicry and play in addition to, and as opposed to, its assigned role in representing another (person, thing).

The power of the page to mimic its betters—a parodic playfulness of the text that Nashe reinscribes at the level of character in Jack Wilton—is initially situated within a context of game rather than earnest:

> But as you loue good fellowship and ames ace . . . it shall be lawfull for anie whatsoeuer to play with false dice in a corner on the couer of this foresayd Acts and Monuments. [Pp. 207–8]

Not only is the given context of *The Unfortunate Traveller* a games context, but its given order is a spurious order of pages:

> Whereas you were wont to swere men on a pantofle to be true to your puisant order, you shall sweare them on nothing but this Chronicle of the king of Pages hence forward. [Pp. 207–8]

The context of game duplicates, but may also threaten to preempt, the "serious" contexts of law (the language of which it parodies), of hierarchical order and ceremony, of martyrology (acts and monuments), and of historical chronicle. The play of the parasitic pages duplicates the world of earnest, the very substance of which it simultaneously absorbs.

In the narrative of *The Unfortunate Traveller*, the page is born guilty. He is conceived in sin in the moment in which Henry VIII forces his way into the French town of Turwin (which "lost her

maidenhood, and opened her gates to more then *Iane Trosse* did"
[p. 209]), and he springs to life as an "ingenious infant," the instant "king of the cans and blacke iackes, prince of the pigmeis . . .
Lord high regent of rashers" (p. 209). The infant affirms himself
and gives promise of a remarkable destiny in a series of tricks in
which he outwits various camp-followers of Henry's campaign. It
is not as an innocent, however, but as a precociously sophisticated
observer that he penetrates the mask of purity worn by those
"coystrell Clearkes (who were in band with Sathan, and not of
anie Souldiers collar nor hatband)" (p. 225). This band of per-
fumed noncombatants who, in washing their hands of the pollu-
tions of the field, "troubled and [s]oyled more water with their
washing, than the Cammell doth" [p. 226] nevertheless defraud
the combatants of their pay, and they are finally driven from the
field by the "stratagemicall" hero. It is the sophisticated self-
consciousness of this hero (and Nashe's reassessment of his earlier
"innocent" performances, no doubt) that enables him to divine
the fraud and to accept as given the guilt that endless handwashing
merely exposes. The page of *The Unfortunate Traveller* is (in both
senses) no longer the innocently sprightly page of Lylyan fiction;
with its new self-knowledge it seemingly acquires a new "character"
and destiny, both of which can be affirmed in the pronoun and
the narrative of the first person.

   At first it might seem as if this destiny is heroic, and as if the
page has become the site of a formidable power-play. There is a
certain epic promise in the performances of the "strategemicall"
infant, and the emergence of an entire pseudo-order of which the
page is king might seem to represent the full enfranchisement of
an inferior order destined to servitude. These heady possibilities—
which correspond to the hubristic moment of the page in *The Unfortunate Traveller*—are presented in the mode of jest-book and
festive-comedy reversal, culminating in the parodic coronation of
Jack as King of the Drunkards and the seeming displacement of
any other form of power. Not for nothing, though, have the early
episodes of *The Unfortunate Traveller* seemed like a false start to
many readers of the work. It is in the very moment of Jack's
triumph that a consciousness of mortality ("the waining of my

youthfull dayes") asserts itself, transforming the page into an "unfortunate traveller," a restless fugitive conscious of his own problematical and threatened identity. Incapable of maintaining his "usurped" power, the page of *The Unfortunate Traveller* can only enact, and trace the consequences of, his own guilty knowledge.

What does this guilty knowledge entail? Among other things, a knowledge of what appearances belie:

> About that time that the terror of the world and feauer quartane of the French, *Henrie* the eight (the onely true subiect of Chronicles), aduanced his standard against the two hundred and fifty towers of *Turney* and *Turwin*, and had the Emperour and all the nobilitie of *Flaunders, Holand & Brabant* as mercenarie attendants on his ful-sayld fortune. [P. 209]

It would be possible to cite precisely such a passage to illustrate the "new alienation" of the 1590s, noting a disenchantment that enables the speaker to see through Henry's martial pretensions, even more devastatingly to see through the façade of the "nobilitie" and to discredit the truth of patriotic chronicles. Inevitably, skepticism about Henry VIII, from which sexual innuendo is not absent, will implicate the Elizabethan order and threaten its self-idealizing mythologies. If one wished to add the concept of satire to that of alienation, it would be possible to observe that encomiastic excess has now become the means of technique of satirical exposure, and that a possibly salutary disenchantment has come to prevail.

The loss of an ideal kingship and true nobility is not objective, however, but coextensive with a gain in sophisticated consciousness on the part of the observer. A revision has been effected. Instead of discrediting kingship as such (or reevoking the "true" ideal) this revision may only reinstate the king whose truth now becomes his tyrannical power and uninhibited will. The king's "advancing his standard" is the prelude to his rape and spoliation of the city, in the aftermath of which "the king of the pages" is born virtually as the parodic alter-ego of that potent tyrant.

The disillusioned observer, in "going beyond" any faith in ideal kingship or noble order, (re)discovers the previously mystified truth of kingship; similarly, the naive chronicler of just monarchy gives way (possibly in the same person) to the sophisticated accomplice of despotic power. The moment of disaffection or penetration becomes at least the prelude to a new and final rapprochement, a development suggested by Jack Wilton's ultimate return to the presence of the king. The gain in critical distance and sophisticated consciousness ultimately confers no unlimited freedom or autonomy (the power of the page remains an image of arbitrary power), but rather subjects the observer to a power stripped of ethical justification. Far from gaining a moral perspective, and still further from enacting a revolutionary break with a discredited order, the alienated observer reconstitutes the truth in an unconscionable form.

All that the liberation from naive illusion may confer is an indeterminate time, space, and power of play in the face of an oppressive necessity. There is no final reversal of priority in favor of pages, but only an indeterminate interlude of the page's autonomy and "usurped" power. The life of Jack Wilton becomes coextensive with his episodic narrative; it is a life constituted by the simplest, even the most arbitrary, process of narrative regeneration (the succession of pages), and by the deferment of closure.

The life of this page therefore remains subject to its own necessities and to those of its world. While, from Nashe's newly sophisticated perspective, the forms of literary innocence appear always already to be vitiated by their naive hubris, their self-allegorizing conceit, and their unwitting corruption, the career of the emancipated page nevertheless remains bound in troubling fashion to deception, to guilt, and even to arbitrary violence. It is the spectacle of violence above all that *The Unfortunate Traveller* presents, and it is the spectacle of unjustified violence that Jack Wilton witnesses shortly after embarking on his foreign travels.

In one episode Jack witnesses the Holy War launched by the armies of established order against the disturbingly innocent Anabaptists, while in another he witnesses the frankly secular conflict between the French and the Swiss mercenaries. The results of these conflicts appear to differ in no significant way, nor do they significantly differ from the result of a bear-baiting game. (Only the Anabaptists expect to receive a sign of divine approval and to prevail by force of innocent enthusiasm.) In one instance, the strife is over when "in one place might you behold a heape of dead mur-thered men ouerwhelmed with a falling Steede . . . in another place a bundell of bodies fettered together in their owne bowells" (p. 231), while in another instance strife ends when "one could hardly discern heads from bullets, or clottred haire from mangled flesh hung with goare" (p. 241). It is precisely this nonsignifying excess of violence that repeatedly confronts the reader of *The Unfortunate Traveller* and that intensifies as the work proceeds. This violence, failing to signify, comes to constitute what Jack Wilton enigmati-cally refers to as "a wonderfull spectacle of blood-shed on both sides" (p. 231).

Threatening to constitute a universal theater of cruelty rather than a theater of God's judgments, this violence comes to appear irreducible, and rhetoric inevitably becomes implicated in its perpetuation. The phrase "wonderful spectacle" begins to suggest the possibility of an aesthetic appreciation of violence, and also specifies a role for the author as producer of violent spectacles; Jack Wilton unmasks himself and discloses his complicity when he stands forth as the *author* of the "tragicall catastrophe" (p. 241), which he and the reader alike have witnessed. Such a development is consistent with his announcement, at the beginning of the "un-fortunate" phase of his travels, that "as at *Turwin* I was a demy souldier in iest, so now I became a Martialist in earnest" (p. 231). A career apparently opens up for the mercenary professional whose martial instrument is the pen rather than the sword.

In embracing such a vocation, Jack would, so to speak, make rhetorical destiny his choice, whether one construes that destiny as a subjection to the requirements of the Elizabethan book trade or in somewhat more theoretical terms. However, if Jack/Nashe cannot finally escape this destiny, he does not immediately em-brace it, but rather deflects from it to engage in more innocent forms of by-play. The moment of decision is postponed while cer-tain benign possibilities are explored.

Much of *The Unfortunate Traveller* may be conceived as a review and critique of alternative roles and styles within the humanist theater—humanism *as* theater—in which Jack attempts to find a place for himself. The mythical scene of this humanism is Wittenberg and its adjuncts, namely Rotterdam and the "Emperor's Court."[8] Nashe presents the spectacle of academic play—orations, disputations, processions, academic drama—as a phenomenon of almost Jonsonian frenzy, self-interestedness, and "dunstical" absurdity. Greeting the Duke of Saxony on his arrival in Wittenberg,

> the heads of their vniuersitie (they were great heads of certaintie) met him in their hooded hypocrisie and doctorly accoustrements . . . a very learned or rather ruthfull oration was deliuered (for it raind all the while) signifieing thus much, that it was all by patch & by peecemeale stolne out of *Tully*. [P. 246]

It is now as an alien presence that Jack Wilton witnesses academic performances (or university wit), yet certain redeeming possibilities remain within that sphere. For one thing, the parodying of formal oratory may become a form of liberating play, a utopian lightening of the formal burden of language. In the bourgeois orator Vanderhulk's welcoming address to the Duke of Saxony on his arrival in the city, a nonsensical extravagance and liberty of speech are achieved:

> O orificiall rethorike, wipe thy euerlasting mouth, and affoord me a more Indian metaphor than that, for the braue princely bloud of a Saxon. Oratorie, vncaske the bard hutch of thy complements, and with the triumphantest troupe in thy treasurie doe trewage vnto him. What impotent speech with his eight partes may not specifie, this vnestimable gift, holding his peace, shall as it were (with teares I speak it) do wherby as it may seeme or appeare to manifest or declare, and yet it is, and yet it is not, and yet it may be a diminitiue oblation meritorious to your high pusillanimitie and indignitie. Why should I goe gadding and fisgigging after firking falantado amfibologies? wit is wit, and good will is good will. [P. 248]

The inspired malapropism that transforms "artificial" into "orificiall" immediately reconstitutes sober Rhetoric and Oratory as Rabelaisian prodigals, big spenders rather than hoarders, while further malapropisms flowing from the loosened tongue of Vander-hulk deny the superior dignity of the listening prince, and sub-stitute for the formal acknowledgment of artificial distinctions a more orificial possibility of egalitarian good will: "Bonie Duke, frolike in our boure.... we wil winke on thy imperfections, drinke to thy fauorites, and al thy foes shall stinke before vs. So be it. Farewell" (p. 249).

What "impotent speech . . . may not specifie" begins to emerge in successive lapses that lead finally to specification of a *common* humanity, a vulgar eloquence, a leveling indecorum. (A release of tension is achieved when the Duke laughs at Vanderhulk's address.) However, such utopian possibilities are not readily available to Jack Wilton, who remains an alienated onlooker. The utopian innocence of Vanderhulk's speech remains as inaccessible in its comic vulgarity as the millenarian innocence of the Anabaptists, constituting a possibility that cannot seriously be entertained by the sophisticated observer.

What constitutes a more serious possibility within the context of Nashe's radically alienated vision is the power of Cornelius Agrippa. Significantly, it is not as a disputant or skeptical philoso-pher that Nashe presents Agrippa in *The Unfortunate Traveller,* but as the re-creator of lost illusions. Drawing to some extent on Agrippa's contemporary reputation[9]—or at least on one aspect of it—Nashe makes Agrippa into an all-powerful magician who domi-nates Wittenberg and the "Emperor's Court" by virtue of his power to stage magical spectacles. No doubt Agrippa's ascendancy may partly be due to the academic humanists' total inability to achieve (let alone conceal) art, yet the sources of Agrippa's power—which depends only secondarily on his unique possession of a magical "perspective glass"—lie deeper within humanism itself.

Before entering Wittenberg, Jack Wilton passes through Rotter-dam, where he observes Erasmus and More closeted together. Jack begins by speaking of them in terms of familiar hyperbole ("learn-ings chiefe ornament," "super-ingenious clarke"), yet these terms become equivocal as he comments on Erasmus's perverse decision to swim with the stream of folly in order to ingratiate himself with

princes. The commendation of More shifts through studied ambivalence ("hee concluded with himselfe to lay downe a perfect plot
of a common-wealth or gouerment, which he would intitle his
Vtopia") to abrupt unmasking: "So left we them to prosecute their
discontented studies" (p. 246). *Utopia* becomes the "perfect plot"
—ideal place, but also subversive design and compensatory fiction
—of the discontented mind conspiring with itself; indeed, in having
"traueld in a cleane contrarie prouince" (p. 245), More is a proto-
typical unfortunate traveler. Erasmus's superingenuity turns back
on itself, facilitating his defeated rapprochement with the folly of
the world.

Jack Wilton's disconcerting punch line ("their discontented
studies") is unaccompanied, however, by any explicit condemna-
tion, and its force lies precisely in its causal acceptance. To the
observer without illusions, a certain "discontent," self-seeking, and
duplicity can be taken for granted even in such exemplary figures
as "aged learning's" chief ornament and "merie" Sir Thomas More.
Only Cornelius Agrippa can supply to the humanist audience,
which includes Erasmus, More, and the humanist Emperor Charles
V and his court, the lost illusion(s) of an ideal humanism. To each
his own image.

While one is satisfied with a view of Ovid and his "hook nose,"
Erasmus, "who was not wanting in that honorable meeting, re-
quested to see *Tully* in that same grace and maiestie he pleaded his
oration *pro Roscio Amerino*" (p. 252), a request to which Agrippa
"easily condescended." The Emperor Charles V prefers the noble
spectacle of the nine worthies, "*Dauid, Salomon, Gedeon,* and the
rest, in that similitude and likenes that they liued vpon earth,"
while More—according to some courtiers talking "to wearie out
the time"—was shown "the whole destruction of Troy in a dreame"
(p. 253). Within a rhetorical humanism perhaps subject from the
start to alienation, ennui, and discontent, the one who finally
emerges supreme is the master of trompe l'oeil and purveyor of
lingering dreams. Beyond any illusion himself, he maintains the
(more or less) noble illusions of others.

Nashe's exaltation of Agrippa, together with his well-established
interest in Agrippa's works, might indeed seem to imply a radical

affinity of the kind suggested by Merritt Lawlis: "A careful comparison of Nashe's works with Agrippa's may reveal a significant meeting of minds."[10] At the narrative level, however, Jack's dramatized encounter with Agrippa, while reaffirming the preeminence of the latter as illusionist, does not result in any permanent attachment or even in any visible emulation. If anything, it results in a minor disappointment. Before entering Rotterdam, Jack has attached himself to the Earl of Surrey, whom he significantly refers to as "my late master" (Significantly in that Surrey rather than Wyatt or Sidney epitomized for Elizabethans the phase of English Petrarchan sonneteering). Jack and Surrey playfully switch identities before entering Wittenberg as spectators, and it is in their reversed identites that they leave the "Emperor's Court," now in the company of Agrippa. It is therefore in the guise of *Surrey* that Jack asks Agrippa to show "the liuely image of *Geraldine, his loue,* in the glasse, and what at that instant she did and with whome she was talking" (p. 254). Predictably, and without penetrating the disguise or sensing any possibly malicious intent, Agrippa displays Geraldine, not as a particularly lively image, but "sicke weeping on her bed, and resolued all into deuout religion for the absence of her Lord." Ravished by this spectacle, the real Surrey breaks out with an "extemporal dity," one in which, however, the limiting principle of Agrippa's art becomes apparent:

> Hir daintie lims tinsill hir silke soft sheets,
> Hir rose-crownd cheekes eclipse my dazeled sight;
> O glasse, with too much ioy my thoughts thou greets,
> And yet thou shewest me day but by twy-light.
>
> [Pp. 254–55, ll. 32–35]

It is precisely in "greeting the thoughts" of others that Agrippa's power and paradoxical servitude consist; the master of illusion remains finally the servant of others' illusions (self-gratifying fantasies). The limitations of Agrippa's magic become doubly apparent when, having conjured up the ostensibly desired image of Geraldine, and having ministered to Surrey's erotic reveries, Surrey "reawakens" to the absence of his mistress and to the ineffaceable difference between "day" and the "twilight" of illusion.

79

What is finally more telling than Nashe's eulogy of Agrippa, his casting of Agrippa in the role of the magician, or even the benign status he assigns to magic, is Jack's dramatized separation from Agrippa in the narrative of *The Unfortunate Traveller.* Almost immediately after Surrey has declaimed his "extemporal ditty," Agrippa simply passes out of the picture. The not ultimately so potent art of the illusionist remains alien to Nashe's genius and also subject to his critical penetration.

What then remains for Jack Wilton?[11] Perhaps only his old relationship, subsequently renewed, with his "late master" the Earl of Surrey. This relationship has long been recognized as a dramatized critique of the Petrarchan style; what needs to be said is that the relation between Surrey and Jack is not one of simple antagonism, which it is commonly taken to be as an anti-Petrarchan parody. The privilege accorded to this relationship in the narrative and the particular incidents within it reaffirm Jack's own statement that he remains inescapably a "nobleman's page." Nashe makes of the relationship an informal essay in the complex dynamics of literary development.

The relationship between Jack and Surrey is evidently a transmutation of the one said to have existed between the historical Earl of Surrey and his servant Pickering, "with whom he was arrested for having broken the windows of certain London houses and churches."[12] While such anecdotes may have suggested the obvious real-life moral that Jack was as good as his master, *The Unfortunate Traveller* goes further in suggesting that there is no essential difference between master and servant. The roles are interchangeable, and for much of the narrative they are interchanged, with Jack masquerading as Surrey and vice versa. The initial humorous complicity between the two in this exchange of roles becomes threatened as Jack persists in his impersonation beyond the limits of the game, and finally, after having passed himself off as Surrey without Surrey's knowing it, he creates a situation in which a public showdown seems probable. Confronted at a public banquet by the "real" Surrey, the feigned Surrey, accompanied by his mistress and playing the part even to excess ("lyke *Anthonie* and *Cleopatra,* when they quafte standing boules of Wine spiced with pearle together" [p. 267]), hesitates momentarily before resigning himself to the mercy of his master. The latter duly plays "his" part in generously overlooking the presumption of his now contrite follower, moved partly by Jack's plea that he has not compromised the integrity of the Earl's character by playing an ignoble part.

However happy this ending, what has become apparent is that no ontological guarantees underpin the respective roles and styles of master and servant. Both roles are arbitrarily constituted, and the peaceful restoration of the *status quo ante* depends on Jack's willingness to submit. What begins in the liberating complicity of play between master and servant, both of whom pass before the world in their feigned parts, moves dangerously close to earnest (as in *Volpone,* the servant's denial that he is the imposter; the master's violent reassertion of "himself") before matters are gracefully resolved. What cannot be restored, however, is the security of a natural hierarchy; conventional priorities must now tactfully be upheld.

What complicates the problem is that something more than a symmetrical opposition of styles is involved. Surrey's part must not only be restored to him, but restored intact. Jack begins to go beyond the bounds in his freely improvised, unauthorized performance as Surrey, and the uncontrollable "slippage'" becomes apparent when, at the climactic moment in Jack's show, he has come more to resemble the noble prodigal Antony than his "late master." Still worse, in publicly flaunting his antiheroine, Diamante (Cleopatra), who has betrayed her husband in order to become his mistress, Jack threatens to rob Surrey not only of his own "character," but of the entire play in which he performs. What this peculiarity suggests is the inadequacy of a merely oppositional concept of literary anti-Petrarchanism; on one hand, conventional priorities are upheld, while on the other the "original" part is usurped by an imposter and expanded, improvised, and transformed to a point at which it ceases to be recognizable. In presenting the relationship between Jack and Surrey, and in presenting the "lively image" of Diamante, courtesan and spendthrift, Nashe attempts to dramatize a process of literary development that cannot be conceived either in terms of simple succession or of simple opposition, though perhaps dialectically.

The poems Nashe gives to Surrey in *The Unfortuante Traveller* are as authentic (nonparodic) as any of their kind; they represent a genuine point of departure in the absence of any other origins than literary ones. Not only would a modern reader find it difficult to single these poems out as parodies in an Elizabethan anthology, but "Surrey's" extemporal ditty did in fact appear in *England's Parnassus* (1600) over the signature "T. Nash." Despite claims to the contrary, it is difficult to see in what way these poems differ from "authentic" specimens of their kind:

> All soule, no earthly flesh, why dost thou fade?
>> All gold, no worthlesse drosse, why lookst thou pale?
> Sicknesse, how darst thou one so fair inuade?
> Too base infirmitie to worke hir bale.
>> Heauen be distemperd since she grieued pines,
>> Neuer be drie these my sad plaintiue lines.
>
> Perch thou, my spirit, on hir siluer breasts,
> And with their pain-redoubled musike-beatings,
> Let them tosse thee to a world where all toile rests,
> Where blisse is subiect to no feares defeatings:
>> Hir praise I tune whose tongue doth tune the sphears,
>> And gets new muses in hir hearers eares.
>
> [Pp. 254, ll. 1–12]

Only in their context in *The Unfortunate Traveller* could these stanzas appear humorously intended in the narrow sense, their new "dislocation" constituting a critical perspective upon them. Indeed, there is no reason to assume that these poems were composed originally for inclusion in *The Unfortunate Traveller;* their incorporation in the narrative under the name of Surrey need imply no more than the achievement of critical perspective by Nashe. Although the poem has a self-parodying conceitedness, it does not differ in that respect from attested specimens of its kind, and the integrity or innocence of the Petrarchan style is always already violated by witty excess. This is precisely the point Jack makes when Surrey, confronted by the attractive and complaisant Diamante, makes her a stalking horse for the absent Geraldine and proceeds to "assault her with rhymes." Observing this ludicrous proceeding, Jack comments: "I perswade my self he was more in loue with his own curious forming fancie than hir face; and truth it is, many become passionate louers onely to winne praise to theyr wits" (p. 262).

At the level of explicit critique it is possible for Jack to recognize the narcissism (also the latent violence) of Surrey as innocent courtly lover and to observe his transformation of the "real" Diamante into the chaste Geraldine of his fancy; Surrey's innocent idealism is a problematical role to which he is wedded. However, this recognition does not disqualify Surrey's poems as a stylistic point of departure, nor does Nashe oppose to those poems the unvarnished truth.

While a desire for such a violent, terminal opposition may be present in Nashe's staging of the relationship between Surrey and Jack Wilton, the full opposition (which could only be philistine) does not materialize. Surrey first confesses his love for Geraldine in a poetical prose to which the word *parody* in its limited sense might apply, but that still represents an undifferentiated art of poesie, not "prose as prose."

> Thou knowest statelie *Geraldine,* too stately I feare for mee to doe homage to her statue or shrine. . . . Her high exalted sunne beames haue set the Phenix neast of my breast on fire, and I my selfe haue brought Arabian spiceries of sweet passions and praises to furnish out the funerall flame of my follie. [P. 243]

To this outburst, which includes a somewhat equivocal account of Geraldine's appointment of Surrey as her "servant," Jack Wilton disconcertingly responds:

> Not a little was I delighted with this vnexpected loue storie, especially from a mouth out of which was nought wont to march but sterne precepts of grauetie & modestie. . . . Now I beseech God loue me so well as I loue a plaine dealing man; earth is earth, flesh is flesh, earth wil to earth, and flesh vnto flesh; fraile earth, fraile flesh, who can keepe you from the work of your creation? [P. 245]

If the plain-dealing man is opposing to Surrey's poeticisms his own version of things ("the prose of the world"), he nevertheless presents that commentary as an understanding of Surrey's cen-sored meaning—as what Surrey confesses in spite of himself. In bringing matters down to earth, he elicits the truth of Surrey's narrative. At the same time, however, he reinscribes Surrey's idealism in an inverted form; it is the very passage I have quoted that John Berryman singles out to exemplify both the typical Nashe of *The Unfortunate Traveller* and Nashe's capacity to write an informal but exalted prose. What takes the place of Surrey's poesie is not mythical plain dealing but an informal prose poem, drawing humorously but gracefully on liturgical cadences. *Earth* and *frailtie*, repeated with indulgent irony, become terms within a visionary perspective upon "the work of creation," a "work" in which both erotic and rhetorical processes are subsumed. Only this work, which entails both the denial and the reinscription of an idea of transcendence, maintains the precarious difference between flesh and the earth to which it would otherwise come right down.

An antiromantic conception may therefore "save" both poetry and the superficially antagonistic relation of servant to master, antistyle to style. An erotic rather than an illusionistic art, even (or especially) when desublimated and made self-conscious, prom-ises to redeem "rhetoric" from its destructive antagonism and negativity, while antiromance offers itself as a viable mode. This mode cannot, however, impose itself on *The Unfortunate Traveller* as a whole, and Jack Wilton, shortly after the speech I have cited above, frustratedly remarks: "Dismissing this fruitless annotation *pro et contra*, toward Venice we progressed" (p. 245). Outside the restricted frame of amorous antiromance, violence, including erotic violence, cannot be denied. The grotesque rape of a saintly matron returns the reader to a cosmic metatheater in which a wild melodrama of rape, murder, and revenge is enacted, and in which rhetoric takes on a manic fury.

What Jack Wilton ultimately confronts, more as a spectator than a leading character, is the apparent irreducibility of violence. A "good" art, which Jack can provisionally identify with the art of healing, for example, or with good advice,[13] cannot ultimately prevail, at least not within the city. Perhaps the most significant instance of good art to appear in the final stages of *The Unfortunate Traveller* is that which Jack witnesses in the banqueting house of a Roman merchant:

> I sawe a summer banketting house . . . builte round of greene marble like a Theater with-out: within there was a heauen and earth comprehended both vnder one roofe; the heauen was a cleere ouerhanging vault of christall, wherein the Sunne and Moone and each visible Starre had its true similitude . . . by what enwrapped arte I cannot conceive, these spheares in their proper orbes obserued their circular wheelinges and turnings, making a certaine kinde of soft angelical murmeringe musike. . . . On the wel clothed boughs . . . were pearcht as many sortes of shrill breasted birdes as the Summer hath allowed for singing men in hir syluane chappels. [Pp. 282–83]

On these justly admired pages, the golden world, the crystal firmament—indeed, a cosmic splendor and divine order—make positively their last appearance, but now translated into pure bourgeois spectacle suggestively located in the theaterlike summerhouse of a city merchant. No correspondence exists between what the "theater" contains and what lies outside it, nor is any return to this now-illusory *status quo ante* envisaged ("except God should make another paradise" [p. 282]). The spectacle has all the additional poignancy of its total unreality, its unearthly trompe l'oeil, no longer representing a conceivable order of things.

The spectacle is now both self-contained and transparent to the initiated eye. Paradoxically, it may take on additional interest on account of the subtle artifice that produces it, and the pleasure of discovery may replace the pleasure of illusion:

> Who though there were bodies without soules, and sweete resembled substances without sense, yet by the mathematicall experimentes of long siluer pipes secretlye inrinded in the intrailes of the boughes whereon they sate . . . they whistled and freely carold theyr naturall field note. [P. 283]

The process of discovery may even suggest, as it does to Jack, the possibility of a divine artificer rather than a creator, yet as knowledge grows more profound it threatens to dispel the charm: "Those bellowes with the rising and falling of leaden plummets wounde vp on a wheele, dyd beate vp and downe incessantly" (p. 284). The sophisticates would ultimately prefer to "renounce coniectures of art" and "say it was done by inchantment" (p. 285).

The inability of this good art to prevail upon the knowing reader or the work as a whole seemingly leaves only one alternative, that of an "art" of ultimate violence. It is such an art—which parodies the melodrama of the Elizabethan theater—that Nashe finally presents. A chain of murder and revenge culminates in the execution of a leading offender:

> Brauely did [the executioner] drum on this *Cutwolfes* bones, not breaking them outright, but, like a sadler knocking in of tackes, iarring on them quaueringly with his hammer a great while together. No ioint about him but with a hatchet he had for the nones he disioynted halfe, and then with boyling lead souldered vp the woundes from bleeding; his tongue he puld out, least he should blaspheme in his torment; venimous stinging wormes hee thrust into his eares, to keep his head rauingly occupied: with cankers scruzed to peeces hee rubd his mouth and his gums; no lim of his but was lingeringly splinterd in shiuers. In this horror left they him on the wheele as in hell. [P. 327]

The section including the execution of Cutwolf is introduced as "a spectacle that will adde to your faith" (p. 320), and the logic of the advertisement is clear: Jack Wilton and the reader alike will bear witness to the ultimate triumph of justice and indeed to the triumph of a moral art. The executioner, skilled in his trade, indulges in no mindless frenzy of violence, but practices a controlled and refined technique of dismemberment. His work may contribute to the victim's spiritual welfare by depriving him of the tongue with which he might otherwise question providence. The victim is even prevented from thinking heretical thoughts as he undergoes his torment. The staged execution, moreover, reconstitutes for those who witness it an image of hell, and thus of a last Judgment. If the image of Eden fails to "adde to your faith," a more powerful image may succeed in its place. A disciplined, moralized, and justified violence may ostensibly end all violence, at the same time reasserting the just providence of an absent deity.

It goes almost without saying that the advertising of the spectacle undercuts its moral pretensions as well as its claims to represent "the promised end." As a tour de force of sadistic excess, the spectacle is indeed "wonderfull," offering intense voyeuristic excitement under an edifying cover. A demonic art, making its appeal to the "fallen" mind, may somewhat insidiously present itself in the image of legality. Stripped of this cover, all that will remain is an art—and ultimately a page—of extreme and calculated cruelty.

The implications of this episode are teasing. On one hand, the executioner, phlegmatically proceeding with his task, represents the appalling "innocence" of a moral art in the service of a postulated ultimate justice, while on the other the conscious advertising of the spectacle undermines this innocence only to leave a "pure" exultant sadism tempting the reader. Again it may seem as if we can choose only between folly and knavery, between naive acceptance of a "justified" or signifying violence and sophisticated acceptance of violence as nonedifying spectacle; in either case, violence remains inescapable, at least within the closed circuit of author and reader. Such is the impasse at which *The Unfortunate Traveller* arrives, and with which it confronts us in our reading. Unable to escape its bondage to a violence that it may ironize but not transcend, the work can offer nothing more positive than a limited perspective on its own processes.

On the narrative level, Jack Wilton, suitably awed by the "trunculent tragedie" to which he has been a witness, marries his "courtezan" and settles down to live on her late husband's fortune. This reformation of character and bourgeois happy ending, parodically akin to those of Deloney's fictions, attest to the moral impact of the execution scene, enabling the book to conclude to the presumable satisfaction of its law-abiding readers, yet we would remain among Jack Wilton's "creditors" if we assumed that anything had constructively been resolved.[14]

CHAPTER 5

RHETORIC AND TRUTH

The troublesome rhetoric to which I referred in the first chapter, and with which I have remained in touch, only becomes troublesome insofar as it is conceived in proximate relation to logic (dialectic) and in ultimate relation to truth, conceived as being on the "side" of logic but ideally independent of it. These relationships are antagonistic and competitive, never balanced or static. Questions of priority are always involved, an ultimate power of representation remains at stake, and no equilibrium is possible while the opposing, but also mutually constitutive, terms may each lay claim to ultimate exclusiveness.

The possibility of absolute mutual exclusiveness is envisaged in the quotation from Newton Garver's preface to *Speech and Phenomena* included in my first chapter. Both logic and rhetoric are conceived as autonomous *systems* of interpretation and representation, one of which must ultimately prove redundant. It is of course possible to reduce the tension arising from this confrontation by reducing both logic and rhetoric to merely instrumental status, and by declining, perhaps with justification, to make the issue a matter of principle. But this delay does not resolve the issue; it merely brackets it. Even in practice, the superiority of one term— one system, one instrument—to the other will continue to be assumed.

As a self-enclosed and all-encompassing system, "rhetoric" claims the power to constitute and evaluate any utterance whatsoever, quite independently of the performer's alleged intentions or commitment to criteria other than those of performance. To the extent that truth remains an issue, it does so perhaps as one rhetorical effect among others—even as the most powerful effect. Outside the system of rhetoric, truth persists only as the *illusion* that rhetorical consciousness dispels; on the inside truth reappears transformed by sophisticated understanding. To become conscious of language, then, is immediately to become conscious of language *as* rhetoric. It is to become conscious of language "always already" contingent, manipulated, and allied to power. (The primitive paradigm of rhetorical manipulativeness, even if self-deception is entailed, is that of the inspired shaman in relation to his community.) "Innocent" or "truthful" utterances of whatever kind will merely be without effect, or else they will produce an effect (may once have produced an effect) that rhetoric assimilates and reproduces at will. No significant (i.e., effective) utterance, including silence itself, escapes the embrace of rhetorical understanding.

The privileging of rhetoric to the exclusion of any competing principle of utterance or interpretation represents a formal or philosophical possibility, yet this is not a possibility extensively developed in the work of Nashe and his peers. Despite some reversals of polarity, local rather than general in extent, what emerges as a more serious possibility is anxiety about rhetorical encroachment or fear of the seemingly inexhaustible (malign, hidden) implications of rhetorical performance. An unconditional emancipation from these forms of anxiety is conceived only, perhaps, in the avowedly religious poetry of the period, into which various liberating theological conceptions can be introduced. Otherwise, romance constitutes the best possibility of emancipation, not from the necessities of rhetoric, but from the accompanying negations of the ideal.

Shakespearean romance in particular may virtually be defined as the *successful* reinscription of the ideal within a rhetoric bound to temporality, to theatricality, and to performance. Such romance ("late" rather than "early") does not seek to bypass rhetoric or to revert to an original condition of linguistic or other innocence, but rather persists until the return of a "lost" ideal transforms the blighted world of which rhetoric has seemed endlessly to speak. With this return, forms of innocence reappear within and beyond sophistication, while seemingly rigid forms and antitheses melt

90

into one another, effecting a release of tension. The war of opposing principles yields to a new harmony, the coming of which is prefigured in *Antony and Cleopatra,* in which two versions of "peace," Caesar's and Cleopatra's, can both establish themselves at the end of the play.

Nothing strictly comparable to Shakespearean romance can, of course, be found in Nashe's work. Nashe's own antipathy to romance as a literary form remains virtually definitive of his career, while, with the limited exception of *The Unfortunate Traveller,* his works are characterized by narrative "blockage," a frenzied stasis of pure performance. (Endless repetition without significant progress constitutes the "hell" of *Pierce Penniless.*) An antipathy even to the available forms of romantic fiction marks Nashe's work, which, despite its fantastic elaboration in some respects, remains parodically bound to forms of literal discourse: the jeremiad, biography, chronicle, and so forth. In few other writers of the period is the sheer force of the literal so strongly acknowledged. Despite the hypertrophy of play in Nashe's work, the emancipating possibilities of romance—its redeeming fictions, its narrative unfolding, its triumphs of love and imagination—are consistently denied to (or by) Nashe.

Despite all this, however, a certain romanticism characterizes Nashe's early conceptions, and antiromance implies at once a negation and a reinscription of romance in a novel form. Such antiromance emerges overtly in *The Unfortunate Traveller,* particularly in the Surrey-Jack episodes. A comparable instance of antiromance is central to *Lenten Stuff,*[1] in which Nashe effects a comic transformation of Marlowe's *Hero and Leander.* (The *un*romantic transformation of the poem, constituting a flat denial of romance, occurs in the puppet theater of Jonson's *Bartholomew Fair.*) In *Lenten Stuff,* too—the narrative kernel of which is Nashe's own enforced flight from London following the prohibition of his satirical play, *The Isle of Dogs*—certain antiromance elements are present. The retreat from the turbulent city to the quiet haven of Yarmouth becomes an informal version of pastoral—a parodic prose idyll—while Nashe's parody of civic assertion in his history of Yarmouth ironically romanticizes the local fishing industry.

"The Praise of the Red Herring" concludes with the return of the grand style as conscious mock-heroic rather than as witless travesty, while the "lost ideal" or romantic myth can now successfully be reinscribed in a comic rather than "serious" form:

> The puissant red herring, the golden *Hesperides* red herring, the *Meonian* red herring, the red herring of red Herrings Hall, euery pregnant peculiar of whose resplendent laude and honour to delineate and adumbrate to the ample life were a woorke that would drinke drie fourescore and eighteene Castalian fountaines of eloquence, consume another *Athens* of facunditie, and abate the haughtiest poeticall fury twixt this and the burning Zone and the tropike of Cancer. [P. 226]

The apotheosis of the red herring is also the apotheosis of a pure rhetoric no longer divorced from or antagonistic to the representation of the ideal;[2] if that rhetoric "draws attention to itself," and even draws attention to its own mechanical processes of repetition, alliteration, and amplification, it can now, having found its proper "theme," afford to do so without prejudice.

What Nashe enacts in *Lenten Stuff,* then, is a sophisticated return to a state of innocence, a "romantic" possibility. This return, however, does not fully liberate rhetoric from its constitutive opposition to logic and even to truth; it even exacerbates that opposition. My principal concern in discussing *Lenten Stuff* will be to consider this opposition as it occurs finally and definitively in Nashe's work. In doing so I shall also consider *Lenten Stuff* as a conclusion, both in fact and in principle, to Nashe's career. Although *Summer's Last Will and Testament* was published in 1600, probably incorporating late additions, it dates from approximately 1592, and may have been published posthumously. *Lenten Stuff,* published in 1599, is normally taken to be the last work Nashe wrote.

Lenten Stuff has always been critically defined as the quintessential Nashean performance or entertainment. It is the work to which the formulas with which I began ("pure style," "saying nothing") virtually apply themselves, while Nashe elevates "themelessness" to a conscious principle. The praise of the red herring substitutes the pseudo-theme for the serious theme that is always lacking, and in doing so achieves a saving grace absent in many of Nashe's earlier performances. Only in the form of the paradoxical encomium, for which he duly cites classical precedents, can Nashe seemingly escape the contradictions of his own position:

> This is a light friskin of my witte, like the prayse of iniustice, the feuer quartane, *Busiris* or *Phalaris,* wherin I follow the trace of the famousest schollers of all ages, whom a wantonizing humour . . . hath possest to play with strawes. [P. 151]

In general, discussions of *Lenten Stuff* are few and unrevealing for the somewhat paradoxical reason that the work *does* so fully represent the quintessential Nashe; its own self-consciousness pre-empts many of the recognitions of latter-day Nashe criticism. A quintessential Nashe is a Nashe rarefied and consciously controlled, diplaying the self-possession that makes *Lenten Stuff* eminently successful as a performance. The conformity of the work to the specifications of the paradoxical encomium tends to rationalize (explain away) "themelessness," removing a primary source of disturbance. The painful self-exposure of such works as *Christ's Tears* and *Pierce Pennilesse* gives way to a new decorousness. All of which makes *Lenten Stuff* a work of self-criticism that largely forestalls "Nashe criticism."

It might still be argued that nothing has fundamentally changed: Nashe continues to ride his peculiar hobby-horses, and the work contains moments of dissonance or alienation as startling as any in the earlier works. Such a discovery, however, might easily be anticipated. What is more to the point is that Nashe's commitment to keeping up appearances, necessitated by the circumstances under which *Lenten Stuff* was produced, has led critics somewhat prematurely to take the work at face value. Despite the superiority of *Lenten Stuff* as entertainment or performance to various other works by Nashe, it neither transcends the contradictions inherent in those works nor finally escapes—though it may attempt to forestall—a confrontation between rhetoric and truth.

Let us begin by recalling that the work was written under circumstances that Nashe dramatizes and that G. R. Hibbard has reconstructed as follows:

> The [*Isle of Dogs*] was . . . completed by the young Ben Jonson, and put on some time in the summer of 1597 before 28 July, when the

theaters were closed. Its performance led an informer to state to the Privy Council that it was "a lewd plaie . . . containynge very seditious and sclanderous matter," and on the strength of this intelligence orders were given for restraint to be put on all the theaters. On top of this, Ben Jonson and two of the players concerned were committed to prison, and Richard Topcliffe, the well-known intelligencer, was given the task of searching Nashe's lodgings and perusing his papers. Nashe, however, appears to have got wind of what was happening . . . and, to use his own words, "was glad to run from" the storm. . . . It would appear that his journey to Yarmouth had been by roundabout ways, to avoid apprehension. . . . But on his arrival there his troubles seem to have ended.[3]

It is difficult to be certain just how serious Nashe's plight may have been. His dramatization of these events in *Lenten Stuff* itself, together with the fact that he did escape and remain unmolested, suggests a certain tolerance or complicity on the part of the authorities. The pursuit of the Marprelate writers and printers reveals a different order of seriousness.[4] At the same time, these events anticipate to a degree the paranoid world in which Ben Jonson, in his poem "On Inviting a Friend to Supper," makes it a point that no spies will be present.

What is certain is that a quick apology and show of good will were required of Nashe. To persist in *this* folly would have been suicidal. Even if he were not to be apprehended, *Lenten Stuff* had to be licensed, and the work therefore begins with apologies and a retraction of *The Isle of Dogs*:

> That infortunate imperfit Embrion of my idle houres . . . breeding vnto me such bitter throwes in the teaming as it did, and the tempestes that arose at his birth so astonishing outragious and violent as if my braine had been conceiued of another Hercules, I was so terrifyed . . . that it was no sooner borne out but I was glad to run from it. [Pp. 153-54]

The speaker's hyperbolical irony suggests, of course, that the apology is feigned—a mock confession that virtually amounts to further self-advertisement. Making a mockery of confession implies a lack of any internalized guilt, while the formal *act* of confession testifies to nothing more than the recognition of a powerful accuser who can be placated in no other way. Confessional performance becomes politically expedient, but the legitimacy of the accusation is implicitly denied by an excess of ostentatious regret. Indeed, the accusation is implicitly reversed. Yet this ironic reversal can never reestablish the essential innocence of the accused, because the very form of mock confession already implies the irrelevance (or power-lessness) of "essential innocence" in a political context in which guilt is constituted by the power of the accuser and located by that power within the accused. To be "really innocent"—and to affirm that innocence—is to be naive about the nature of guilt and about the likelihood that the accuser will allow himself to be in-criminated. The accusation can be made to stick. Moreover, since the conception of essential innocence offers no refuge, an acknowl-edgment of guilt cannot simply be *pro forma;* what is confessed will constitute the guilt of the accused, its precise nature specified by the binding terms of the confession. All that can perhaps be attempted is a form of plea-bargaining, in which the accused settles for somewhat reduced charges. The terms of the confession in *Lenten Stuff* appear to conform to this legalistic necessity, and they predetermine the nature of the work.

What the speaker of *Lenten Stuff* confesses to is not the produc-tion of a seditious libel, but the production of bad art. Since no text of *The Isle of Dogs* is available to us, it is futile to speculate about the nature of the play, although its satirical character can reasonably be assumed. The "badness" of *The Isle of Dogs*—its tempestuous disruptiveness and heroic disproportion—is at once an offense against public order and aesthetic decorum; this "badness" is revealed to the author only after the work has been launched into the world. No good intentions are powerful enough then to "save" the work, nor is it possible for the author to assert the essential integrity of his design, since even that must be recognized as the product of "idle houres." The work must be disavowed as an alien monstrosity, the production of a sorcerer's apprentice rather than of a responsible master. If the speaker is "innocent," that is the source of the problem rather than a justification of his work.

No doubt this confession reflects little more than the necessities of the situation, yet even as a matter of form it constitutes an *acceptance* of guilt that cannot be retracted. Our reading of *Christ's*

Tears may suggest that there is a basis to the speaker's conception of his own guilt; the violation of aesthetic propriety and public "decencie" is the "crime" of the overreaching novice. The denial or avoidance of further guilt, whether at the level of appearances or at a deeper level, becomes the imperative of *Lenten Stuff.*

Perhaps for this reason, the work defines itself as an inconsequential trifle, which is what "lenten stuff" literally means. A denial of "seriousness" or heroic ambition is implicit in the form of the paradoxical encomium, while the main task undertaken in the work consists in scaling down Marlowe's *Hero and Leander* to the dimensions of the mock-heroic. At one point the speaker even extols the craft of the toy maker:

> There is a mathematicall Smith or artificer in Yarmouth that hath made a locke and key that weighes but three farthings, and a chest with a paire of knit gloues in the till of it, whose whole poise is no more but a groat; now I do not thinke but all the Smiths in London, Norwich, or Yorke (if they heard of him) would enuy him, if they could not outworke him. [P. 189]

The ingenuity of the provincial craftsman, which is barely separable from ingenuousness, expresses itself in the form of pure technical virtuosity without threatening implications. The production of exquisite trifles becomes a wonder in itself, and remains so because the "artificer" inhabits a noninvidious world beyond the reach of suspicion or resentment. An opposition thus emerges in *Lenten Stuff* between art forms of guilty excess or violent disproportion and others of harmless wit or diminutive inoffensiveness, with the speaker evidently situating himself on the "side" of the latter. What remains to be forestalled, however, is the power of readers to determine otherwise of the work than the author intends.

The first reader whose response the speaker of *Lenten Stuff* seeks to forestall is a naive one, who seriously misconstrues the work. The author cannot be held responsible for such misconstruction:

> My readers peraduenture may see more into it then I can; for, in comparison of them, in whatsoeuer I set forth, I am . . . as blinde as blinde Bayard, and haue the eyes of a beetle: nothing from them is obscure,

they being quicker sighted then the sunne, to spie in his beames the
moates that are not, and able to transforme the lightest murmuring gnat
to an Elephant. [P. 220]

The reader whose activity is foreseen here may without stretching
the point be called naively logocentric. Installing himself at the
author's expense in the one privileged vantage point from which
the truth may be seen, and at the same time presuming to remain
inscrutable, such a reader arrogates to himself a power of divine
cognition and penetration ("quicker sighted then the sunne"). This
assumed super-vision not only enables the reader to distinguish
between the author's illusion or deceit concerning his own work
and its reality, but to reconstitute that work as an object of serious
understanding rather than of just appreciation. Nothing more is
required by this reader than a "natural" perception of the truth.

It might be said that in foreseeing this reader, Nashe preempts
his reading; Nashe also denies the power of such a reader to see
without being seen. In transforming what the author intends to be
no more than trifle into "an Elephant," this reader can only un-
wittingly repeat the process of the paradoxical encomium, thus
turning game back into earnest in ludicrously solemn fashion. In
opposing this "reader," however, Nashe—or his authorial persona[5]
—displays a certain hesitancy, if not confusion. First, there is the
punning conflation of pagan and Christian logocentrism (sun-Son),
and then there is an apparent misconstruction of the motes and
beams in the relevant Christian parable. (The "beams" of the parable are not sunbeams, and the motes are not flecks of dust in the
sunlight.) Finally, a "misapplication" of the parable occurs.

Ostensibly both irony and parable apply to readerly hubris, a
condition in which the reader presumes to know better than the
author does. What creates the very possibility of such hubris is a
logocentric mythology in which truth is constituted both outside
of performance (appearances) and in opposition to it. Yet no
"demythologization" is effected, nor is the authority of truth
finally overthrown. On the contrary, the speaker betrays a certain
inconsistency in reinvoking the myth.

It would seem as if, in principle, what applies to the reader,
should also apply to the author (authorial persona); insofar as the

privileged perspective is denied to anyone, it is denied to everyone. What would seem necessarily to follow from the dethronement of the hubristic reader is a recognition of common human limitation, and perhaps of the lack of *any* power of divine cognition. Yet in applying the parable of the motes and beams, the speaker accuses the reader, not of failing to see the beam in his own eye while noticing the mote in the eye of another, but of seeing motes where they are not. In other words, the speaker becomes a being of a different order from the reader, identifying himself with the divine narrator (Christ) rather than the mortal subjects of the parable. The reader is dethroned only to have his place usurped—more than usurped—by the speaker himself. This speaker thus assumes the double guise of performer *and* reader, establishing the superiority of his own self-understanding to that of any (naive?) reader. Attempting to assume full control over his own performance and preemptive authority over its interpretation, the speaker becomes his own ideal reader, constituting the "truth" of his own performance.

Instead of pausing at this point to consider the implications of this episode, I shall proceed to a second instance in which an encounter with "the reader" is foreseen. Again a return of/to truth appears to be precipitated by the intervention of the reader, only in this instance the intervention occurs at the level of political actuality rather than of romantic myth. In the first confrontation with the reader, "truth" is the product of true perception (an omniscient perspective) and of pure understanding untroubled by "human" limitations or imperfections. In the second confrontation with the reader, truth can only be the product of a political process of the utmost dubiousness. *Lenten Stuff* was written under suspicion, as we have seen, yet it seems ironically to invite further suspicion: "O, for a Legion of mice-eyed decipherers and calculaters vppon characters, now to augurate what I mean by this" (p. 218). The rhetorical form of this statement remains ambivalently poised between appeal and scorn: a "scornful appeal."

At one level, *Lenten Stuff* is committed to keeping up innocent appearances and must therefore forestall suspicion. It must also forestall a vicious circle in which divination of a hidden meaning, decipherment, and arbitrary resolution constitute the *political* truth. The "legion of mice-eyed decipherers and calculators" now comprises not only naive readers but all potential readers of the text, which must maintain itself in a condition of full alertness. Every reader is incipiently a "spy."

Nashe's antagonism to this form of scrutiny (as distinct from appreciative acceptance) of *Lenten Stuff* gathers force in his attack on informers (pp. 218–19). Adopting the necessary fiction that the good ruler is misled and victimized by self-serving informers, Nashe describes the following "hypothetical" situation:

> Some foole, some drunken man, some madde man in an intoxicate humour hath vttered hee knewe not what, and they, beeing starued for intelligence or want of employment, take hold of it with tooth and nayle, and in spite of all the wayters, will violently breake into the kings chamber, and awake him at midnight to reueale it. [p. 218]

Against this abuse there is no defense but a kind of counter-espionage:

> Say that a more piercing Linceus sight should diue into the intrailes of this insinuating parasites knauery; to the strapado and the stretching torture hee [who?] will referre it for triall, and there eyther teare him limbe from limbe, but hee will extract some capitall confession from him. [Pp. 218–19]

The divining parasite can be opposed only by a more profound diviner, yet the issue must still be "referred" to torture, since the product of divination is not the self-evident truth. However superior the insight of a Linceus, he can operate only within the same *political* structure as the "insinuating parasite," and—whatever Nashe's intentions—the difference between the two is effaced by a characteristic ambivalence of pronoun antecedents. The only truth that can prevail is that which is arbitrarily determined to be true within a structure of political power.

The absurdity and injustice of this situation are fully evident to the speaker of *Lenten Stuff:* "The poore fellow [who?] so tyrannously handled would rather in that extremitie of conuulsion confesse he crucified Iesus Christ then abide it any longer" (p. 219). To put an end to the pain, the victim, whether "parasite" or Linceus, will confess to anything; the more outrageously heinous the crime, the more it may be hoped that it will satisfy the torturer. Again, a kind of mock-confession becomes necessary, testifying to the power of an external agency to establish the guilt of the victim. What is striking, however, is the nature of the crime to which the victim confesses. Within a Christian culture, there is a moral sense in which this confession is always a priori *true;* sin constitutes at least guilt by association with the crucifiers of Christ. However arbitrary the initial accusation, the a priori presence of guilt tends to justify the proceedings in which it is ultimately revealed. Moreover, the extorted confession may be the one "saving" admission capable of reestablishing the truth of the victim's condition. What follows from this truth is the victim's need to be forgiven and his release from the need to keep up appearances. In both his confrontations with anticipated readers of *Lenten Stuff,* then, Nashe reveals—or stages—the inescapable "return" of/to truth. The attack on informers paradoxically tends to justify their role and also to justify the political structure in which the truth of guilt is brought to light, perhaps as the only truth conceivable in, or constituted by, a world of appearances.

The antagonism between literary performance and "reading" continues to parallel that between rhetoric and truth—a truth not to be denied. The speaker in *Lenten Stuff*—the "I" who declaims the praise of the red herring—tends thus to remain self-divided or to be located ambivalently on the "side" of performance or that of reading. No final escape from the constitutive opposition between rhetoric and truth appears possible. While the outrageous claims of "truth," whether conceived in mythical or political terms, justify a continuing impenitence on the part of the performer, the very fact of continuing performance "logically" implies self-alienation and concealed guilt, both of which call for confessional self-exposure. The presence of this bind necessarily makes *Lenten Stuff* inconclusive, or at least brings Nashe to the limits of his own enterprise. Beyond this point there may be nothing further to conclude about Nashe's work. (Nashe falls silent after *Lenten Stuff,* and by 1601 he is reported to have died.)

From the standpoint of modern criticism of Renaissance literature, I would suggest that Nashe's career reveals some of the dilemmas of his "rhetorical" contemporaries and that his repeated staging of the scandal of authorship exposes some of the lacunae in a highly idealistic "Renaissance" conception of literature. If Nashe has fully been recognized as a performer and as a representative figure of his time, perhaps further recognition is due to him as a significant anatomist of Elizabethan literary performance.

APPENDIX

Canon and Chronology of Nashe's Principal Works (in order of publication)

The Anatomy of Absurdity   1589
    Railing monologue on contemporary "abuses"

Preface to Robert Greene's *Menaphon*   1589

An Almond for a Parrot   1590
    Humorous pamphlet written in "folly" style against "Martin Mar-
    prelate"

Pierce Pennilesse, His Supplication to the Devil   1592
    Railing satire including a discourse on the Seven Deadly Sins and
    a beast allegory

Strange News   1592
    Humorous pamphlet attacking Gabriel Harvey

Christ's Tears over Jerusalem   1593
    Didactic tract in which the fall of Jerusalem prefigures that of Lon-
    don should the city persist in its evil ways

The Terrors of the Night   1594
    Popular tract on demons, spirits, and oppressive anxieties of the
    night

The Unfortunate Traveller or The Life of Jack Wilton   1594
    Fictional memoirs of an itinerant page

Have with You to Saffron Walden   1596
    Humorous pamphlet against Gabriel Harvey

Lenten Stuff   1599
    Mock-encomium on the "red herring," including a parodic retelling
    of Marlowe's "Hero and Leander"

Summer's Last Will and Testament   1600
    Play based on pageant of the seasons, a version of which was prob-
    ably acted in 1592

"The Choice of Valentines"   n.d.
    "Scandalous" poem on the dildo

NOTES

CHAPTER 1

1. C. S. Lewis, *English Literature in the Sixteenth Century* (New York: Oxford University Press, 1954), p. 416, and Richard A. Lanham, "Thomas Nashe and Jack Wilton: Personality as Structure in *The Unfortunate Traveller*," *Studies in Short Fiction* 4, no. 3 (1967): 202.

2. "Historical explanations," whether given in the context of ideas, of academic rhetoric and English prose style, of economic and social development, of the emergence of printing, or of politics are not lacking. Detailed citation is impossible here, but see for example R. M. Stevenson, "The Duality of Thomas Nashe" (Ph.D. diss., Duke University, 1972); Walter F. Staton, "The Significance of the Literary Career of Thomas Nashe" (Ph.D. diss., University of Pennsylvania, 1955); G. R. Hibbard, *Thomas Nashe* (Cambridge: Harvard University Press, 1962); and Travis Summersgill, "The Influence of the Marprelate Controversy on the Style of Thomas Nashe," *Studies in Philology* 48 (April 1951): 140–60.

3. While I do not intend to center my discussion on Nashe's roles, I recognize the inseparability of "rhetorical" authorship from role-playing, of performance from persona. Nashe's roles include authorial ones played on the stage of the world, such as those of Cuthbert Curry-knaves in *An Almond for a Parrot* and of Pierce Pennilesse in the work thus entitled; they also include such quasi-dramatic roles as those of Will Summer in *Summer's Last Will and Testament*, of Christ in *Christ's Tears over Jerusalem*, and of Jack Wilton in *The Unfortunate Traveller*. It would seem on the face of it more suitable to approach Nashe's literary career as a series of rhetorical situations (or "contracts") than it would be to approach it as a sustained attempt to "say" something. What comes first, in other words, is not the imperative of truth or of signification but rather the socially constituted opportunity or necessity to perform. From a historical point of view, it is appropriate to recognize Nashe's reshaping of authorial "personality" to accord with the particular conditions of Elizabethan book-making and -selling; it is also appropriate to recognize Nashe's conscious and historically "timely" attempts at self-inscription within impersonal rhetorical conventions. These historically significant developments,

not exclusively associated with Nashe, have generally been recognized. Perhaps it will suffice to cite in this connection G. R. Hibbard, *Thomas Nashe.*

4. In Nashe's version of the quarrel, his "innocent" reference to Harvey as the son of a provincial ropemaker was enough to fuel all subsequent hostilities.

5. Gabriel Harvey in his *Works*, 3 vols., ed. A. B. Grosart (London: Huth Library, 1885; reprint ed., New York: A.M.C. Press, 1966), 1: 222-23.

6. *The Works of Thomas Nashe*, ed. R. G. McKerrow, 5 vols., (London, 1904-10); reprint ed. F. P. Wilson (Oxford: Basil Blackwell, 1966), hereafter referred to as *Works.*

7. "McKerrow's edition" is legendary in its own right, somewhat at the expense of "Nashe's works."

8. *Works*, 5: 76-110. In fairness it must be admitted that McKerrow is combatting simplistic legends about the quarrel between Nashe and Harvey, and may also be reacting to the partisan absurdities perpetrated by Grosart in his introductions to Harvey's works.

9. Lanham, "Thomas Nashe and Jack Wilton," p. 216.

10. Richard A. Lanham, *The Motives of Eloquence* (New Haven: Yale University Press, 1976). Despite the title of this book, the question of motives (of motivation, or of a lack of rational motivation) is barely touched upon.

11. Newton Garver, preface to *Speech and Phenomena* by Jacques Derrida, trans. David B. Allison (Evanston: Northwestern University Press, 1973), p. xi. The summary relegation of grammar to the realm of the trivial is obviously not uncontentious.

12. Nowhere is this clearer than in *The Motives of Eloquence*, in which "extremes" of seriousness or levity are pronounced "sociopathic." The need is thus preemptively established for a diagnostic and coercive pseudo-science.

13. It would, of course, be unjust to imply that Fish remains fixed in a single position, or that his early work on Milton and on seventeenth-century prose represents his present position.

14. Stanley E. Fish, *Self-Consuming Artifacts* (Berkeley and Los Angeles: University of California Press, 1974), p. 365.

15. Admittedly, Saussure's conception of the sign seeks to preclude any possibility and to eliminate any site of "division" or of *différance,* just as it denies autonomous right or autonomous existence to signifier and signified. Derrida, however, suggests that the division Saussure locates outside of speech —in inscription—is ineradicably present within the structure of the sign.

16. See Hans-Georg Gadamer, *Philosophical Hermeneutics,* trans. D. R. Linge (Berkeley and Los Angeles: University of California Press, 1976), pp. 12-13: "As a student of Plato, I particularly love those scenes in which Socrates gets into dispute with the Sophist virtuosi and drives them to despair by his questions. Eventually they can endure his questions no longer and claim for themselves the apparently preferable role of the questioner. And what happens? They can think of nothing to ask."

17. Stanley E. Fish, *Surprised by Sin* (Berkeley and Los Angeles: University of California Press, 1971).

18. I refer to some programmatic passages in Derrida, notably in *Of Grammatology*, trans. Gayatri Chakrovorty Spivak (Baltimore: Johns Hopkins University Press, 1976), pp. 6–7, and "Structure, Sign, and Play in the Discourse of the Human Sciences," in *The Structuralist Controversy: The Languages of Criticism and the Sciences of Man*, ed. Richard Macksey and Eugenio Donato (Baltimore: Johns Hopkins University Press, 1972), p. 264. The significance of these passages has, however, been overemphasized (or distorted) by repeated quotation out of context.

19. The significance of "play" within the Renaissance can obviously not be dealt with in this summary fashion, a liability that my general argument cannot wholly escape. See, however, Mikhail Bakhtin, *Rabelais and His World*, trans. Hélène Iswolsky (Cambridge: M.I.T. Press, 1968); C. L. Barber, *Shakespeare's Festive Comedy* (Princeton: Princeton University Press, 1972); Robert Weimann, *Shakespeare and the Popular Tradition in the Theater: Studies in the Social Dimension of Dramatic Form and Function*, ed. Robert Schwartz (Baltimore: Johns Hopkins University Press, 1978); Natalie Zemon Davis, *Society and Culture in Early Modern France* (Stanford: Stanford University Press, 1975); and Johan Huizinga, *Homo Ludens* (Boston: Beacon Press, 1978).

20. Recent works that, without referring directly to Shakespeare, introduce considerations highly pertinent to our reading of the Shakespearean canon include Patricia Parker, *Inescapable Romance* (Princeton: Princeton University Press, 1978), and Jonathan Goldberg, *Endlesse Worke* (Baltimore: Johns Hopkins University Press, 1981).

21. The connection is usually established in terms of word-coinage, yet larger affinities between the prose of Nashe and that of Shakespeare have also been recognized. Shakespeare's possible indebtedness can be tracked in the footnotes to the Arden Comedies and Histories. See also Jürgen Schäfer, *Documentation in the O.E.D.: Shakespeare and Nashe as Test Cases* (Oxford: Clarendon Press, 1980).

22. For example, Summersgill, "The Influence of the Marprelate Controversy"; George Minor Anderson, "The Use of Language and Rhetoric in Nashe's *The Unfortunate Traveller*" (Ph.D. diss., Yale University, 1961); and G. R. Randolph, "An Analysis of Form and Style in the Prose Works of Thomas Nashe" (Ph.D. diss., University of Florida, 1962).

23. John Berryman, introduction to *The Unfortunate Traveller* (New York: Putnam, 1967), pp. 7–29.

24. Coleridge in *Biographia Literaria*, 2 vols., ed. J. Shawcross (Oxford: Clarendon Press, 1907), cited in Berryman's introduction to *The Unfortunate Traveller*, p. 18.

25. Merritt Lawlis (ed.), *Elizabethan Prose Fiction* (New York: Odyssey Press, 1967), p. 440.

26. Jonas Barish, *Ben Jonson and the Language of Prose Comedy* (New York: Norton, 1960), p. 1.

27. Jonas Barish, "The Prose Style of John Lyly," *ELH* 23 (1956): 25.

28. Rosemond Tuve, "'Imitation' and Images," in *Elizabethan Essays in Criticism,* ed. Paul Alpers (New York: Oxford University Press, 1967), p. 50.

29. It is a commonplace that Nashe begins his career as a prose author by observing a stilted academic decorum and by appealing to an ideal audience of learned readers. He then consciously popularizes his writing. There is no loss of rhetorical self-consciousness in this process, although practicing an art of sinking costs Nashe many pangs. See especially *The Anatomie of Absurditie,* in *Works,* 1:1-50.

30. Precisely because of Nashe's early identification of good style with aristocratic good breeding and good order in society: "I am not ignorant how eloquent our gowned age is grown of late; so that euery mechanicall mate abhorreth the English he was borne to, and plucks, with a solemne periphrasis, his *vt vales* from the inkehorne" (Preface to *Menaphon,* in *Works,* 3:311). Here "decorum" is putatively aristocratic and hierarchical, as it appears necessarily to be in Tuve's account. Nashe, however, qualifies this elementary conception in due course.

31. George Puttenham, *The Arte of English Poesie* (1589), ed. Gladys Doidge Willcock and Alice Walker (Cambridge: At the University Press, 1936), pp. 261-62.

32. It might be argued that the entire problem I have outlined is therefore artificial and that the presence of "rhetoric" is always contingent. To make this argument, however, is to relapse into the classic discourse of the sign.

CHAPTER 2

1. This postponement occurs partly because once morality play has given way to theater, representation itself tends to emerge as a preemptive rather than a subsidiary concern.

2. This commonplace is developed in original and significant terms by Joel Altman, *The Tudor Play of Mind* (Berkeley and Los Angeles: University of California Press, 1978).

3. Once the nature of that "mind" is irreversibly acknowledged, a psychology—or at least a degree of psychological sophistication—is emphatically called for. The theory of melancholy goes some distance toward satisfying the need, although it retains idealist presuppositions.

4. Hence it becomes possible to discuss Nashe to a large degree, as others have done, in "anti-" terms: antiheroic, antiromantic, antipastoral, and so forth, yet more than simple antagonism is involved.

5. The Gorgias who, along with his disciples, is exposed in the Platonic

dialogue that goes under this name, but also the Gorgias whose surviving fragments remain mere curiosities.

6. Hence, as McKerrow suggests, some of his antagonism to the "progressive," Ramist, Harveys.

7. Roger Ascham, *The Schoolmaster*, in *English Works*, ed. W. A. Wright (1904); reprint ed., Cambridge: At the University Press, 1970), p. 265.

8. Quite soon Ben Jonson accuses Spenser of writing a nonidiomatic language, and the complaint recurs in the twentieth century in relation to Milton's poetry.

9. For the details of Nashe's career in the trade, see, among others, Staton and Hibbard, but also *The Three Parnassus Plays* ed. J. B. Leishman (London: Ivor Nicholson & Watson, 1949).

10. In his own terms, G. R. Hibbard registers the peculiarity, in both senses of the word, of *Christ's Tears:* "It is, it seems to me, far and away the worst thing Nashe ever wrote. Neither trivial nor dull, it has about it all the fascination of the positively and thoroughly bad. It could have been written in no other time. . . . Those features of Nashe's work that are most characteristic and typical of him and his age are here carried to lengths of excess that render them either ridiculous or revolting. . . . *Christ's Tears* is a monument of bad taste, literary tactlessness and unremitting over-elaboration for which it is not easy to find a parallel; a kind of gigantic oxymoron in which style and content, tone and intention are consistently at odds" (*Thomas Nashe* [Cambridge: Harvard University Press, 1962], pp. 122–23).

11. Preface to *Menaphon*, in *Works*, 3:311.

12. *Works*, 1:183. If I deal rather summarily with this point, it is because the allegory of Pride represents the "medieval" Nashe, whereas the Nashe I am more concerned with is the Renaissance figure who tries to redeem style from this allegorical necessity. I would also suggest that the allegory of Pride is a more central problem, for example, to Spenser than it is to Nashe, who remains uncommitted to allegory and thus not fundamentally obliged to confront Pride as the *true* subject of any allegorical art.

13. Jonas Barish, *Ben Jonson and the Language of Prose Comedy* (New York: Norton, 1960), pp. 62–89 and passim.

14. Hibbard (*Thomas Nashe*, p. 32) notes the emergent "I" as a significant feature of this preface.

15. In this context *humor* may be taken to incorporate its normal range of Elizabethan meanings, including those of arbitrary physiologico-intellectual disposition and changeability of mood. *Humour* remains a term antithetical rather than parallel to *wit* in Nashe's usage, yet the implied mobility of humor may enable it to escape the rigidification to which wit becomes subject in the works of Lyly and Greene. One point that cannot be ignored in any consideration of Nashe's "extemporall" doctrine is its continuing academicism: "The frequent necessity of having to answer opponents in argument . . . fostered the

ability to extemporize. Quintilian's *Institutes of Oratory* was a basic text for the study of rhetoric in Nashe's day, and in it extemporaneousness is constantly extolled" (Travis Summersgill, "The Influence of the Marprelate Controversy on the Style of Thomas Nashe," *Studies in Philology* 48 [April 1951]: 155).

16. Barish, *Ben Jonson and the Language of Prose Comedy*, p. 49.

17. *An Almond for a Parrat*, in *Works*, 3:339–76. For accounts of this conflict see, among others, McKerrow, in *Works*, 5:65–109, and Leland H. Carlson, "Research on Martin Marprelate," in *English Satire*, ed. Ronald Paulson and Leland H. Carlson (Los Angeles: Clark Library, 1972), pp. 3–48.

18. These were powers of which Nashe himself utlimately became one victim. His own works and those of Gabriel Harvey were prohibited by decree of Bishops Whitgift and Cooper in 1599, in the course of a more general attempt by church and state authorities to suppress works deemed libelous, disaffected, or inimical to public order. Assuming that Nashe had indeed been enlisted by these same bishops to oppose Martin Marprelate, the irony inherent in these later developments is both self-evident and open to political thematization.

19. Including the strong argument that such leveling schemes stop inconsistently short of their logical conclusion, namely the millenarian communism (or "primitive Christianity") of the Anabaptists. They stop short, Nashe alleges, as soon as established property rights are threatened.

20. Isaak Walton, *Lives*, World's Classics, no. 303 (Oxford: Clarendon Press, 1962), p. 199.

21. On the Marprelate conflict as festive comedy, see C. L. Barber, "The May-game of Martin Marprelate," in *Shakespeare's Festive Comedy* (Princeton: Princeton University Press, 1972), pp. 51–57. See also Raymond Anselment, *'Twixt Jest and Earnest: Marprelate, Milton, Marvell, Swift and the Decorum of Religious Ridicule* (Toronto: University of Toronto Press, 1980).

22. Among the novel features of Marprelate's performance (novel in the context of religious polemic) was his introduction of a typographical dialogue between the margin and the center of the page. A new abusive voice, speaking quite literally from the margin, assails the inviolate space and episcopal decorum of the center. Marprelate's moment of indecorum was a moment only, however, preceding the attempt to establish a new discursive legitimacy and a new decorum of "plain style."

23. G. R. Hibbard, *Thomas Nashe* (Cambridge: Harvard University Press, 1962), p. 45.

24. As a profound though highly idealized treatment of this motif, Huizinga's *Homo Ludens* remains indispensable.

25. *Pierce Pennilesse his Svpplication to the Divell*, in *Works*, 1: 137–246.

26. *Christ's Teares ouer Ierusalem*, in *Works*, 2: 1–186.

27. *Works*, 1: 319: "When I was a little ape at Cambridge, I thought [*Euphues*] was *ipse ille*."

CHAPTER 3

1. See, in addition to those works already cited, Louis B. Wright, *Middle Class Culture in Elizabethan England* (London: Methuen, 1964).

2. *The Anatomie of Absurditie*, in *Works*, 1: 5–50.

3. The topos of the Seven Deadly Sins is prominent in both *Pierce Pennilesse* and *Christ's Tears*.

4. The most popular of Nashe's works in his time, *Pierce* evoked spurious sequels, established Nashe as a "personality," and mythologized the plight of the artist-wit in the clutches of cruel patrons and mercenary printers.

5. Nashe's melancholy is definitively evoked by C. S. Lewis: "I think every reader will suspect that [Nashe's] 'burliness' is by no means the whole story: may indeed only be the 'manic' peak balanced in private by a 'depressive' trough. The *Terrors* is ostensibly a sceptical work written to remove night-fears. And Nashe gets great fun out of the minor devils of whom 'infinite millions will hang swarming about a worm-eaten nose'.... But these, like nearly all Nashe's comic images, are comic only if you see them in a flash and from exactly the right angle. Move a hair's breadth, dwell on them a second too long, and they become disturbing" (*English Literature in the Sixteenth Century* [New York: Oxford University Press, 1954], p. 414).

6. The bizarre figure of endless verbal repetition with variation that definitively characterizes Christ's speech may represent the apotheosis of rhetoric, its final sublimation. Although C. S. Lewis considers this device unprecedented, it is akin to the figure of *traductio* that occurs in Arcadian prose.

7. Nashe's invocation becomes a parodic tour de force: "Mine owne wit I cleane disinherite; thy fiery Clouen-tongued inspiration be my Muse. Lende my wordes the forcible wings of Lightnings, that they may peirce vnawares into marrow and reynes of my Readers ... file away the superfluous affectation of my prophane puft vp phrase, that I may be thy pure simple Orator" (p. 15).

8. In the "strong" version of Elizabethan poetics—that represented by Sidney's *Apologie*—ideal poetic order does not follow from ideal pastoral order, but rather constitutes it. In doing so, poetic "making" remains an image of the divine creation of a "golden world." Although the poetic act is thus nominally underwritten by divine example, a curious reversal is incipient. The mere existence of poetry, and of the creative power of the poetic "wit," begins to emerge as "no small evidence" of the actuality of a prelapsarian world, and thus of the truth of revelation. Within a skeptical world, poetry thus tends to constitute, not derive itself from, an original mythic moment of creation. Despite its fictional character, poetry becomes primary evidence of a truth for which other evidences have failed. A failure of poetry would, therefore, have profound repercussions. This point is highly pertinent to an understanding of Nashe.

9. In terms of my general argument, the city might have its rhetoric but no true poetry.

10. Such a reaction may also account for the "romantic revival" within which those plays have their place, and which is marked by a revival of interest in the romances of the 1580s.

11. Nashe transgressed in writing *The Isle of Dogs*, a play suppressed after its first performance and subsequently lost. This event, along with Nashe's subsequent flight to Yarmouth, supplies the narrative framework for *Lenten Stuff*. See G. R. Hibbard, *Thomas Nashe* (Cambridge: Harvard University Press, 1962), p. 235-37.

12. See E. D. Mackerness, "'Christ's Tears' and the Literature of Warning," *English Studies* 33 (December 1952): 251-54. This literature is far more extensive than Mackerness suggests, and the destruction of Jerusalem becomes a common prefiguration of London's fate.

13. The ambivalent play of words in *Christ's Tears* breaks down every saving distinction of persons, as it tends to do in all Nashe's works. What contributes to Nashe's difficulties in the representation of the Messiah is the perplexity of the rhetorically educated over the "low style" of the Bible. (See C. S. Lewis, "The Literary Impact of the Authorized Version," in *Selected Essays*, ed. John Hayward [Cambridge: At the University Press, 1979], pp. 126-45.) Although this perplexity can be traced back at least to Augustine, in Nashe's particular case it involves a suspicion of Christ's "resembling himself to the similitude of the meanest," which can only imply cosmic hubris. In this "similitude," moreover, divinity cannot be recognized and will eventually have to unmask itself.

14. "Pleasant approach" is synonymous, for George Puttenham, with an ideal decorum. See *The Art of English Poesie*, ed. Gladys Doidge Willcock and Alice Walker (Cambridge: At the University Press, 1936), pp. 261-62.

CHAPTER 4

1. The primacy of figures tends to be implied in the notion of rhetoric.

2. The question of Nashe's historical role as a coiner and compounder, as well as of the reliability of *O.E.D.* first citations, has interestingly been discussed in Jürgen Schäfer, *Documentation in the O.E.D.: Shakespeare and Nashe as Test Cases* (Oxford: Clarendon Press, 1980). While the innovativeness of the Elizabethans may generally have been overestimated, Nashe's innovativeness appears to have been underestimated in relation to Shakespeare's.

3. A. J. Kirkman, *TLS*, 4 May 1962, p. 325, cited in Merritt Lawlis (ed.), *Elizabethan Prose Fiction* (New York: Odyssey Press), p. 439.

4. Nashe is directly referring to the books of journeymen-translators, from

the banality of which his similar work is ostensibly saved by his innovative brilliance.

5. The *Vnfortunate Traveller or The Life of Iacke Wilton*, in *Works*, 2: 198–328.

6. See Agnes M. C. Latham, "Satire on Literary Themes and Modes in Nashe's *The Unfortunate Traveller*," *English Studies*, n.s. 1 (1948): 85–100.

7. See, in addition to works already cited, standard histories of the novel and Fredson Bowers, "Thomas Nashe and the Picaresque Tradition," *University of Virginia Studies* 1 (1941): 12–27.

8. Nashe anticipates readers for whom Wittenberg "means" Luther and the German Reformation. Luther makes a brief appearance as a low-comedy buffoon, scolding without grace or wit.

9. See Charles G. Nauert, *Agrippa and the Crisis of Renaissance Thought* (Urbana: University of Illinois Press, 1965).

10. Lawlis, *Elizabethan Prose Fiction*, p. 484. The "significant meeting" has, however, been recognized since McKerrow extensively traced Nashe's indebtedness in his edition.

11. Critics have suggested that Aretino functions as an exemplary character in *The Unfortunate Traveller*. Nashe's paradoxical ideal of the literary careerist and terrorist, bound neither to his own nor others' illusions, is an ideal at once libertine and libertarian. Aretino becomes a figure of unique power and glamor, the uncompromising redeemer of a base trade, and the liberator of Jack Wilton from bondage in the narrative. Perhaps this heroism lies beyond the reach of Jack Wilton, the lying page.

12. *DNB*, cited in Lawlis, *Elizabethan Prose Fiction*, p. 475.

13. Jack is impressed by the well-conducted Roman hospitals and by the advice given to him by an English gentleman that he return whence he came.

14. G. R. Hibbard resolves the situation by refusing to think the unthinkable: "I find it inconceivable that any Elizabethan, and least of all that conventionally-minded defender of the Anglican Church, Thomas Nashe, should write of God's justice and its inexorable working in a manner which has anything to do with burlesque. A phrase such as 'fasten your eies on this spectacle that will adde to your faith' puts the matter beyond all doubt" (*Thomas Nashe* [Cambridge: Harvard University Press, 1962], p. 176).

CHAPTER 5

1. *Nashes Lenten Stuffe*, in *Works*, 3: 144–226. G. R. Hibbard's comment may be taken to summarize the general response: "It is the most idiosyncratic and, in some ways, the most brilliant of all Nashe's writings" (*Thomas Nashe* [Cambridge: Harvard University Press, 1962], p. 236).

2. The perils of the rhetorical ascent, perhaps into delirium, continue to be registered in *Lenten Stuff*.

3. Hibbard, *Thomas Nashe*, p. 235.

4. See Leland H. Carlson, "Research on Martin Marprelate," in *English Satire*, ed. Ronald Paulson and Leland H. Carlson (Los Angeles: Clark Library, 1972).

5. In reverting to *propria persona* in *Lenten Stuff*, Nashe opens up once again a confusing double discourse of self and persona. A distance between the speaker and the self in *Lenten Stuff* is never established as a constant, and the "I" of this work remains unfixed. It is of course possible to read *Lenten Stuff*, like other works by Nashe, as the dramatic monologue of a "crazy" speaker, a style of criticism that has been practiced with limited results in the case of Swift.

The Johns Hopkins University Press

Unredeemed Rhetoric: Thomas Nashe and the Scandal of Authorship

This book was composed in Aldine Roman text and display by Horne Associates, Inc., from a design by Alan Carter. It was printed on S. D. Warren's 50-lb. Sebago Eggshell paper and bound by Universal Lithographers. The manuscript was edited by Jane Warth.